BISTRA JOHNSON

DOWN THE LOIRE GRAPEVINE

Or

The Indispensable Guide to Renaissance France –
make the most of your visit to the Loire châteaux

The Valois Saga in 9 chapters
9 Kings and 9 Ladies
determine the fate of a country and
change its landscape with their magnificent castles

First published 2010
This edition 2011

Copyright © Bistra Johnson 2010

The right of Bistra Johnson to be identified as the Author of this Work has been asserted by her in accordance with the Copyright, Designs and Patents Act 1988

Cover design © Bistra Johnson

All rights reserved. No part of this publication may be reproduced, stored in a retrieval system, or transmitted in any form or by any means, electronic, mechanical, photocopying, recording or otherwise without the prior permission in writing of the publisher.

ISBN: 978-0-9556875-2-5

To my father

*who taught me to appreciate architecture and
who never lost his enthusiasm for the subject*

Bistra Johnson is a writer and translator who lives in Paris with her husband.

Also by Bistra Johnson in Lulu:
"Thracian Princess"
"Tales from the Future"

CONTENTS

PREFACE	6
INTRODUCTION:	8
The Valois Dynasty in the Loire Valley (14th – 16th century)	8
The Capets, the Plantagenets and the rest	10
A Feudal France (14th century)	16
Chapter 1: A Queen, a Dauphin, a Bastard and a Maid	18
Chapter 2: The Beauty and the Beast	40
Chapter 3: The Bourgeois Gentleman	45
Chapter 4: France Marries Brittany, Round 1	56
Chapter 5: France Marries Brittany, Round 2	64
Chapter 6: The Chivalrous King	69
Chapter 7: The Rule of the Huntress	82
Chapter 8: The Florentine in Power	89
Chapter 9: The War of the Three Henries	102
APPENDIX	115
Loire. The River. The Vineyards.	115
The Châteaux of the Loire	119
Royal Genealogy	134

PREFACE

Once upon a time Kings, Queens and Princes lived happily in fabulous castles spread across a beautiful river valley… Forget the fairy tales! There *is* a valley which still preserves the memory of a whole Royal Dynasty and it is called The Loire Valley! The stories about the Valois Royals in the Loire Valley are far more entertaining than any compilation of fairy tales Charles Perrault might have come up with. Perhaps you do know Charles Perrault and his Tales of Mother Goose, but it's doubtful that you are aware that he got the inspiration for Sleeping Beauty's castle from a château where he stayed in the Loire valley, or that the Bluebeard character is loosely based on a companion of Joan of Arc who fought alongside her at Orleans.

But this is not going to be a history lesson. Instead let's take a walk along the river and indulge ourselves in say a wine-tasting tour or even a treasure hunt? Don't rush to get your spade though. The Valois were much more sophisticated than that; refined Renaissance aristocrats wouldn't do something as unimaginative as to bury their valuables underground. They wanted to show off and to leave something behind for future generations to admire and to remember them by. The châteaux they built and the art work they commissioned is the best legacy they could think of. These masterpieces still remain there along the Loire, outliving those who owned them.

Sailing down the Loire can be like sailing back in time. We find ourselves in a time-warp, in an enchanted place. Over the roar of the gushing waters of the big river, we suddenly become aware of the distant echoes of past battles, of grandiose building works, of the sound of hunting horns.

But let's not think about those long and boring history lessons we had to put up with at school. Let's steal a look between the dry historical facts and we'll find some fascinating human stories to match the reality shows we watch today.

Behind the splendid facades of the grand palaces, life went on pretty much the same way as today, and if we are curious enough to look more carefully, we might catch glimpses through the layers of time of what went on in the sumptuous salons.

A friend once asked me why I was so fascinated with Renaissance châteaux. "They are oppressive, he argued, they express power." That might be so, but if it wasn't for those rich and powerful patrons of art, the artists never would've been given the chance to demonstrate what they were capable of. Creating art for the sake of art is very noble, but even artists have to earn their keep!

What they left behind is truly amazing and we are fortunate enough that time has spared all those works of art for us to admire today. However in order to appreciate them fully we should be looking at them in the context of the historical period they belong to, the Renaissance.

We might also ask why exactly the Loire valley had become such a magnet for the royals and the nobility. Why not Paris, the capital of France? Let's find out.

INTRODUCTION

The Valois Dynasty in the Loire Valley
(14th – 16th century)

With the final battles of the Hundred Years War winding up, France finally felt at ease and opened its doors to the Renaissance, which was already flourishing in neighbouring Italy. The monarchs from the Valois Dynasty certainly appreciated the Italian artistic styles and were eager to introduce them at home.

Gradually the fortified châteaux in the Loire valley, their favoured residences, were transformed into pleasure palaces, following the new architectural trends, surrounded by luxurious gardens and boasting the finest examples of art and design money could buy. This was the golden age of the Loire valley.

The warrior Kings of the past gave way to more refined and educated monarchs, patrons of the arts, literature, music. They surrounded themselves with humanists, poets, musicians, architects, artists, landscape designers etc. and gave them the chance to develop their talents.

The rest of the aristocracy, no longer feudal Lords, determined not to be outdone, also built palaces following the example set by the Kings.

And despite this being allegedly a male-dominated era, there were quite a few women, who left their mark. Joan of Arc shone on the military field, but there were others who influenced politics, literature, arts. Their role has often been underestimated, but nonetheless one can't fail to notice their presence.

François I, the Prince of the Renaissance said: "A court without women is like a garden without flowers." He was a lady's man and made many conquests. Today his remark might sound a bit sexist. Yet, he probably saw more in women than just their beauty. His mother and his sister certainly had an influence on him; and both of them were accomplished, well educated women. But there were many others before and after them.

From Joan of Arc (The Maid of Orleans) till the murder of Henri III, the last Valois King, French history has been made in the Loire country. A Royal seat from the time of Charles VII till the captivity of François I, it remained a favourite retreat for the nobility till the end of the Valois reign.

Henri II and his mistress, Diane de Poitiers, his Florentine wife, the formidable Catherine de Medici and her children, they all spent time in the Loire valley and left their mark.

Henri III had to flee back there when Paris was held by the Catholic League. The end of King Henri III's reign marks also the end of an era. It was the end of the Valois Dynasty, for Henri III died, leaving no heir to the French throne.

The crown then passed to his cousin Henri de Navarre, who became known as Henri IV, *"le Vert Galant"*, the first of the Bourbon Dynasty, who changed his religion six times; the one of "Paris is well worth a mass" fame (*"Paris vaut bien une messe"*). No surprise he will settle in the capital, while Louise of Lorraine, the inconsolable widow of Henri III will retire to Chenonceau and live there till the end of her life in apartments, entirely furnished in black…

Chenonceau and the rest of the Loire châteaux, so favoured by the Valois, will fall into oblivion during the Bourbon era that follows.

The Capets, the Plantagenets and the rest
or how it all started

England and the connection between the English and French Royals; the end of the Capets and the ascent of the Valois; the beginning of the Hundred Years War.

A Slice of History (you can skip this bit)

A word of advice from me – when you write a book, you should never ever digress like this, because it will just confuse your reader who is probably confused anyway. You should start from the beginning, that is from one point and then follow the events that unfold in a chronological order. But in for a penny, in for a pound! I have broken a lot of rules already, so I'll break this one too.

Besides from my 21st century watch tower I can take the opportunity to rewind the tape of history, to enlarge the image a bit and have a really good look...

It's important to clarify a key point about the 100 Years War – how did it come about?

From history textbooks, we are left with the impression that the 100 Years War was a war between England and France; which is a bit farfetched. True, English troops were heavily involved and so were the Scots – on the other side of the conflict. And then the 100 Years War is not even a war in the true sense of the word. It consists of a series of rather sporadic armed conflicts, which later historians will refer to as "The 100 Years War".

In those feudal times people had a different mentality. There wasn't a centralised power neither in France, Britain nor the rest of Europe. Even the Kings had a very limited influence, and some of their "vassals" might at times become dangerously powerful. The story of the famous Magna Carta is a case in point.

Territories would often change hands and have yet another overlord, depending on the political situation of the moment.

In fact The 100 Years War (14th -15th century) was a war for supremacy between two, even three branches of the same royal family fighting for the same crown – the French one. The main protagonists are the English Royal House of Plantagenet extraction (the so called *Angevin* line), their French cousins, the Valois, who had ascended to the French throne after the last direct Capet died without a male heir and whose daughter was married to the English King and lastly the Burgundy Branch of the Valois Dynasty, also legitimate pretenders to the crown.

The House of Plantagenet (originates from the county of Anjou, Loire Valley, 12th century) feels affinity with France and is in fact French by its nature. The language they speak is of course, French.

Henry II Plantagenet (the founder of the Plantagenet line) himself is the son of Geoffroy IV, Count of Anjou, and the granddaughter of William the Conqueror. He is born in Le Mans (a city in the Loire valley), marries the rich heiress Eleanor of Aquitaine, recently divorced from the French King Louis VII Capet and furthermore that lady brings to her new husband a splendid dowry – the whole of Aquitaine (south west of France); after which the said Henry Plantagenet proceeds to become the King of England!

Interestingly it would be at **Beaugency** in the Loire valley where in 1152 a Council annulled the marriage of Eleanor and Louis VII of France! This event had a disastrous effect for France in the long run. Eleanor did not give a male heir to her first husband Louis VII, but produced five male and three female children from her second union. After a rather tumultuous marriage, both King Henry II and his Queen Eleanor died in the Loire country in France (Henry II – in **Chinon** and Eleanor – in the abbey of Fontevraud). Some hundred and fifty years later a great-great grandson of theirs, an English King from this same Plantagenet/Angevin Dynasty would get involved in the 100 Years War for the French throne.

Their legendary son, Richard the Lionheart, actually did not have a male issue (or any children in fact). His elder brother Geoffrey, who died at a tournament, left a son, Arthur; however after Richard's demise, their youngest brother John (Lackland) waged a war against Arthur, the legitimate heir to the English throne, killed him and became King John II of England.

Richard the Lionheart was brought up in France and lived there for most of his life (apart from two brief sojourns across the Channel and his gallivanting across the continent on crusades to the Holy Lands and back). He jealously kept his possessions in France and at one time waged a war against his own father, when the latter wanted him to hand over Aquitaine to his brother John.

During his travels, while in Cyprus, Richard married Berengaria, the heiress of Navarre and so added another province to his French possessions. Richard the Lionheart despite his glorious reputation might not have been such a good King to his English subjects, preferring to use his kingdom as a source of revenue to support his armies, but at least he ensured their continual presence on the continent; after all, the empire he inherited, was in actual fact a family estate.

On his way back from the Holy Lands, Richard was captured near Vienna by the Duke of Austria. He was held in captivity for more than a year and in the meantime his brother John Lackland was conspiring against him with the French King Philippe-Auguste. As a result, the strong fortress of **Loches** on the Indre River in the Loire valley, passed, amongst others, to Philippe. On his return Richard forgave John, but came to blows with Philippe over his lands.

According to the legend, **Loches** was taken after a siege of only three hours. Philippe would retake it 10 years later, but his siege would last a whole year!

Richard eventually died in the Limousin, suppressing a revolt led by the Viscount of Limoges. At the time of writing, the château where they say he drew his last breath, has not only survived the great Crusader-King, but, managed to keep up with the times and, despite its medieval appearance, boasts under floor heating, remote control gates, high speed Internet and is up for sale with a price tag of 17 million pounds!

Richard the Lionheart is buried in the abbey of Fontevraud, in the county of Anjou (in the Loire valley), together with his parents and his sister-in-law, Isabelle of Angouleme, the wife of John Lackland. Precisely the offspring of Isabelle and John would continue the Plantagenet/Angevin line.

John Lackland had a bad reputation, perhaps undeservedly, for he was a good administrator and spent more time in England. And yet it was he, who lost most of his family's French possessions (Anjou-Maine-Touraine, Brittany, Normandy, nearly all Poitou, most of Gascony) by the spring of 1205, although he managed to re-conquer Gascony and part of Poitou by 1214.

In 1215 the English Barons and their Scottish and French allies were in such a strong position, as to dictate terms to the King and force him to sign a document, the famous Magna Carta, limiting his power in England. No feudal King in his right mind would willingly agree to the clauses it contained, so it is no surprise that soon afterwards the King renounced the agreement and started war with the Barons; that is pillaging the countryside and laying it to waste.

From a modern point of view that might sound appalling, but let's not forget that we are still in medieval Europe and that was a normal way of conducting warfare, along with the sieges and the invasions. When we read about the *chevauchée* of so and so, we should not be thinking about a pleasant ride on horseback somewhere in the countryside, despite what we have found in the French/English dictionary. The *chevauchée* is a particular term used to indicate precisely burning and pillaging the territory to create havoc and weaken the enemy.

The Barons had to do something if they didn't want to be discredited and lose the loyalty of their subjects, so they invited Prince Louis, the son and heir of the French King Philippe-Auguste and proclaimed him King of England. A contemporary chronicler states that Louis was invited to invade in order "to prevent the realm being pillaged by aliens."

King John held on; he obtained the support of the Pope (who had Louis excommunicated) and fought valiantly. His siege of Rochester castle, which the rebel Barons had taken, is proof of his resolve. He employed 5 siege engines to undermine first the curtain wall and then the keep, causing one of the towers to collapse by supporting it on wooden props, liberally applied with pigs' fat, and then setting them on fire. The defendants kept going, but finally had to surrender due to starvation. He took back the castle (which undermined people's faith in such fortifications) and imprisoned his opponents.

Although King John died the following year, Louis was not able to hold out and losing the support of the Barons, he had to sign a peace treaty and withdraw back to France. John's nine year old son was crowned under the name of King Henry III.

Now, again from a modern point of view, what the Barons did - inviting a foreign prince to invade the land, is nothing short of treason. Yet at the time, this was pretty much common practice.

The term "patriotism", which comes from Greek and means love for one's country, should not be taken as a synonym for "nationalism" today and even less in those times when the term "nation" was still somewhat hazy. The concept of a "nation", both political and cultural, the way we understand it today, emerges about the time of the French revolution. "For King and country" was yet to be coined as an expression of the sentiments of those defending their own.

People in feudal Europe were just expected to be loyal to their overlord. For his part the latter was supposed to protect them in case of war. But land was changing hands so frequently as a result of wars, marriages, inheritance, swaps or other deals and was so often pillaged by friends and enemies alike, that ordinary people often found themselves between the devil and the deep blue sea. No doubt they were used to it and, in order to ensure their succession, they took good care to produce as many children as possible.

Life was cheap then. And expendable. And so it went on and on. The next couple of centuries brought little change. But now it is time to skip a hundred years or so and cross to the other side of the Channel.

A Feudal France
(14th century)

We can imagine the territory of France in those times like a patchwork, changing its patterns all the time, in line with the various interactions of the overlords.

When Philippe IV the Fair (*Philippe Le Bel*), the handsome and audacious French King, disbanded the Order of the Knights Templar, to whom he owed loads of money, and burned their Great Master on the stake, he could hardly have dreamed of the chain of catastrophic events that this was to entail. He had attempted to create a centralised state and rule with an iron hand. The Pope at that time was just a pawn of his, and did not object to the dissolution of the Knights Templar Order on the accusation of heresy.

According to a contemporary chronicler, the Great Master, while burning on the stake, cursed the King with the following words:
"God knows who is wrong, and who has sinned, and woe will come to those, who have condemned us wrongly. God will revenge our death. Lord, know that in truth, all those that have wronged us will suffer because of us."

In fact marrying off his sister Margaret to the English King Edward I and afterwards his own daughter Isabelle to Edward II, son of that couple, Philippe the Fair paved the way for what was to follow.

By divine retribution, or an overambitious plan that went wrong, a sequence of disasters descends afterwards upon the royal family, which eventually leads to the extinction of the line of the Capets. Those events are immortalised by the French writer Maurice Druon in his bestselling series of historical novels.

Les Rois Maudits (the Accursed Kings), as the sons of Philippe the Fair became known, rule one after the other for a period of about 14 years (1314 -1328) and following the death of the third one, Charles IV, the French crown is claimed by their cousin Philippe, who was to become King Philippe VI, the King Found (*le "Roi Trouvé"*), the first from the *Valois* Dynasty. He is the nephew of King Philippe the Fair and takes precedence over the grandson of the latter, Edward III, King of England, according to some very ancient law, that favours the male line (Edward III is the son of Edward II of England and Isabelle of France, the daughter of Philippe the Fair). It is this that ultimately led to the Hundred Years War (1337-1475). It started and continued on and off for over a century, giving an excuse for plunder, looting, violence, all this accompanied by the Black Death.

But we are not going to dwell on it any more. There is plenty on this topic elsewhere for those wanting to know the details. We'll concentrate on the events, leading up to the end of this brutal conflict and the dawn of the Renaissance in France.

We will go back to the Loire country and see what was happening there at the beginning of the 15th century. How come the Loire valley found itself at the heart of a feudal struggle?

CHAPTER 1

A Queen, a Dauphin, a Bastard and a Maid (15th century)

They were a motley crew, the first three, and yet between them they managed to reshape the map of France. Historians are usually tempted to attribute it all to Joan of Arc, but the Maid appeared like a supernova to brighten the political sky and swiftly disappeared, while the other three were there for a very long period and they certainly didn't stay idle.

Together they plotted, together they fought for years and years till they accomplished what they had set out to do. Yet they couldn't be more different. The King is said to have been weak and squeamish, the Duchess – clever and beautiful and the Bastard of Orleans, often referred to as the handsome Dunois (*le beau Dunois*) – brave and charismatic.

The Royal Château of Chinon: Rising high above the town, overlooking the Vienne River, the fortress, built initially by the Count of Blois, Thibaut, reminds us of a time when the history of France and England were intrinsically linked. In the 12th century Henry Plantagenet and Eleanor of Aquitaine held court there and left their imprint on it. The French King, Philippe-Auguste, took the castle from John Lackland in 1205 and built the Coudray keep. With Charles VII a new page of its history opens. He was still just "the little King of Bourges" when he installed his court here in 1427.

Le Carillon de Vendôme – a contemporary *comptine* (a nursery rhyme) goes as follows :

My friends,
What is left

For the gentle Dauphin?
Orleans, Beaugency,
Notre-Dame de Cléry,
Vendôme, Vendôme !

> *Mes amis,*
> *Que reste-t-il*
> *A ce Dauphin si gentil ?*
> *Orléans, Beaugency,*
> *Notre-Dame de Cléry,*
> *Vendôme, Vendôme !*

Enters Charles VII, at the time still the Dauphin or rather the so called "little King of Bourges"(*"le petit roi de Bourges"*), a pejorative nickname, given to him because he holds court in that city, while the throne of France, that should have been rightfully his, is offered to the English King Henry V, the husband of his sister. His lands are reduced to the size of a handkerchief, just the cities quoted in the nursery rhyme above. But is Charles really the weakling, persuaded by Joan of Arc to go to Reims to be crowned? And how did he become the man, who against all odds, succeeded to the French throne?

Charles VII was the son of Charles VI of France and Isabeau of Bavaria; born in 1403, he was the eleventh child of the couple out of a total of 12.

A few months earlier another child was born, a boy named Jean, who was to play a crucial role in the life of the future King Charles VII. Jean was the illegitimate son of Mariette d'Enghien. The father of the boy was no less than the brother of King Charles VI, Louis, the Duke of Orleans himself. And what was more, he acknowledged the child and entrusted him to the care of his wife, Valentina Visconti, to be brought up with her own children.

Now, that made Charles - the son of King Charles VI - a cousin to Jean of Orleans. Unless of course there was some truth in the ugly rumours, spread about at the time, that the Queen Isabeau also had a liaison with her brother-in-law, the Duke of Orleans, and that it was actually him, who had fathered young Charles. If this was indeed the case, young Charles and Jean would be half brothers, sharing the same father.

But let's stick to the facts. King Charles VI of France was much loved by his people and that gained him the name *Charles Le Bien-Aimé* (Charles, the much beloved). However later on people started to call him *Charles le Fol* (Charles the Mad), when in 1392 in the forest of Le Mans (in the Loire country), he attacked his own troops in a fit of madness and killed four men before he was restrained.

He regained his faculties afterwards, but till the end of his life, he suffered from bouts of insanity and this left the country in disarray and a playground for the intrigues of the Regents and the other claimants for the throne.

A Council of Regents was created, presided over by the Queen, Isabeau of Bavaria, where two opposing figures were disputing for power: the brother of Charles VI, Louis, Duke of Orleans and his uncle, Philippe the Hardy, Duke of Burgundy.

There was another uncle Jean, Duke of Berry, the renowned patron of the arts, who built castles and commissioned an illuminated manuscript which is now world famous - The Very Rich Hours of the Duke of Berry, one of the most important pieces of art in history; exquisitely executed, it gives us a unique glimpse into that period (it depicts scenes of life at court and the surrounding countryside with castles in the background, presented in full architectural detail).

All the above mentioned Princes were involved in the government of the kingdom.

Louis of Orleans was a lady's man and had numerous affairs; Isabeau, the Queen of France might've been one of them and probably that's why she supported him against his uncle.

When Philippe the Hardy died in 1404, his son Jean the Fearless (*sans Peur*) became the Duke of Burgundy in his turn.

He insinuated that his cousin, the Duke of Orleans, had made advances to his wife - and cousin of the Queen - Jacqueline of Bavaria. Whether this was true or not, is anybody's guess. A big scandal erupted, which probably aimed to turn the Queen against her protégé.

The Duke of Berry endeavoured to play the role of a peacemaker between his two nephews and tried everything to reconcile them.

The Duke of Orleans was not going to give up easily. He succeeded to remove his cousin's supporters from the Council, thanks to the backing of the Queen.

Desperate to keep hold of his position, his cousin, the Duke of Burgundy, simply hired an assassin to eliminate him. This deed was duly accomplished in 1407.

Widowed, a distraught Valentina Visconti went to Paris and demanded justice. Jean, the bastard son of the late Duke, still a young boy, accompanied her. She was fond of him and is said to have remarked that he should have been hers, that none of her own children was up to the job of getting revenge for the death of his father, like him. She didn't get very far in her petitions to the King. After her death, only a year later, Jean, the Bastard of Orleans, stayed with his half brothers.

He would've been playmates with his cousin Charles, the son of the mad King, who was the same age as him. It's very likely that the Dauphin associated himself with his Orleans cousins from that time.

Being an illegitimate child, didn't put Jean at a disadvantage. In those times the morals were such, that the bastard children of the nobility – and the term was not meant at all in a pejorative sense – enjoyed almost the same privileges and status as their legitimate siblings (even if they were not supposed to inherit their parents).

They were even allowed to use the coat-of-arms of their respective families, provided that they marked their status by imposing the so called *bend* on the shield. Jean's shield will be "Azure, three fleurs-de-lis Or, a label Argent, overall a sinister *bendlet* Sable" (for those not familiar with the Heraldic terms, it means: 3 golden lilies with a silver-white, tri-pointed, horizontal stripe above them and a narrow black diagonal stripe across on a blue background).

Jean's half brother, presently the Duke of Orleans, was related by marriage to the Armagnacs. If his mother didn't obtain justice in her lifetime, he thought he would contrive to get it by other means. This is how the war between Armagnacs and Burgundians was unleashed. The Burgundians had close links with the English…

After the death of the English King Henry IV, his son Henry V inherits the English throne. He coveted the French throne as well, so he decided to marry the daughter of Charles the Mad and thus to get nearer his goal. But he had to go to France and get his bride.

In the meantime young Charles, the future King of France, lived in the court at **Angers** with his prospective parents-in-law Louis II and Yolande d'Aragon, respectively the Duke and the Duchess of Anjou, and his fiancée Marie of Anjou. The Duke of Anjou had already aligned himself to the Orleans/Armagnac clan against the Burgundians.

The château of **Angers,** built initially by the formidable Foulque Nerra, Count of Anjou, an ancestor of Henry Plantagenet and rebuilt by St. Louis in the 13th century, is a veritable fortress, able to withstand any siege, but inside the thick dark grey walls of schist, the Duke and the Duchess had created a more modern Royal residence, also a residence for the Chatelaine, a second chapel…it became in fact almost like a city within the city.

14th – 15th century was a golden period for **Angers**, because the Dukes of Anjou, enlightened Princes and art lovers, enjoyed a dazzling court life at the château. The time they spent in Naples as crowned monarchs, influenced not just their lifestyle but also their conception of architecture.

To this day the château houses the world renowned Apocalypse tapestry. Commissioned in 1375 by Louis I, Duke of Anjou, and probably completed by 1382, this hanging was soon recognised as being exceptional not just in terms of its size (100m/4,5m) but also its stylistic and artistic qualities. The tapestry depicts the last book of the Bible, written by St. John at the end of the 1st century. There are also many interesting details reflecting life at the end of the 13th century, when the country was in the throes of the 100 Years War.

In 1415 Henry V, King of England advanced onto French soil; the French, Armagnacs and Burgundians alike, united at last, fought side by side at the battle of Agincourt to stop the English. The French had the advantage in numbers, but it is the English, who eventually win the battle.

Charles I, Duke of Orleans, who participated too, was captured by the English and remained in London as a prisoner of war for the next 25 years.

The Duke of Berry had managed to persuade King Charles VI of France not to take part in that battle, reminding him of the fate of his own father, King Jean II of France, years ago at Poitiers, when he had been captured by the English. Due to his efforts King Charles VI and his sons avoided a similar fate. The Duke died soon after the battle. Later on his nephew Charles (the future King Charles VII) would inherit his title and the Duchy of Berry.

The war with the English didn't put an end to the rivalry between the Burgundians and the Armagnacs. With Charles I, Duke of Orleans out of the way, his father-in-law, Bernard of Armagnac took things into his own hands. No diplomat, he brought the wrath of the Queen upon his head after he executed a protégé/lover of hers. She was forced to flee and where did she find refuge? Where else, but with the Duke of Burgundy himself!

At about the same time, in the spring of 1417, Yolande d'Aragon became a widow. The fate of the Duchy of Anjou was now in her hands; so was the fate of her son-in-law.

The Duke of Burgundy knew how to use the situation to his advantage. In 1418 he took Paris and massacred the Armagnacs, including their leader, Bernard of Armagnac. He let his allies, the English, take control of the city.

Charles, who has become by then the Dauphin (since the recent death of his elder brother), narrowly escaped the massacre and found refuge in his Duchy of Touraine in the Loire valley. Things seemed very grim indeed for him and for his cause.

The Burgundians were hardly his friends for he sympathised with their arch enemies, the Armagnacs. Paris was in the hands of the former (well, in the hands of their allies, the English), while the young Dauphin was forced to flee and move from one castle to another.

The territory of France was roughly divided into two with the Loire the line of division; the territory to the North of the Loire was held by the English, who also had Aquitaine (the south west corner); the provinces to the South were still faithful to the Dauphin.

Tours (the capital of Touraine) was in the hands of the Burgundians though and Charles failed to retake it. It was not surprising therefore that while passing through **Azay**, a village near **Tours** on his way to **Chinon**, he was insulted by the Burgundian guard there (the village had aligned itself with the Burgundians). As a result, the fortress was taken, the place was burned and the Burgundian captain of the guard and his soldiers were executed there and then.

Hence the village became known as **Azay-le-Brulé** (the burnt) till later times (18th century) when it acquired the name **Azay-le-Rideau** (after lord Ridel d'Azay, who built the 12th century fortress there).

Years later when things calmed down, Charles VII, now King, authorised the rebuilding of the town and a town wall to protect them. One of the most attractive châteaux of the Loire was built there during the time of François I by a wealthy financier and so **Azay** rose from its ashes.

It's unlikely that the **Azay** massacre was carried out because of sheer vindictiveness. The young Prince was known for having a supposedly weak character and a repugnance to violence. At the time he was just 15. Chased out of Paris by his enemies, disinherited by his own parents, the world must've looked to him a very cruel place.

Azay after all was his, a village located in his lands and if its residents had sided with his enemy – a treasonable act, their punishment was not so unfair as it might seem. These were harsh times.

Whatever the situation, Charles was not short of loyal friends. For a start, there was his mother-in-law Yolande d'Aragon, not only the Queen of four kingdoms (Sicily, Naples, Jerusalem and Aragon), but most importantly, the Duchess of Anjou, for the other titles were effectively in name only. She was also the Countess of Provence. This remarkable lady acted as a surrogate mother to Charles. Yolande held court usually in **Anger** or **Saumur** (it was the time of the so called "itinerant" courts).

Saumur isn't such a formidable fortress as **Angers**, but never the less it is strategically situated, commanding the Loire, it is solid and yet elegant, decorated like a country mansion with sculptured machicolations and window balustrades. Yolande d'Aragon must've felt comfortable and safe there.

The Duchess was one of those brilliant women, who played a significant role in shaping the history of France.

It is said that when his natural mother Isabeau sent for Charles, on the demise of his elder brother back in 1417, to take his place in court as the Dauphin, Yolande replied to her: "We haven't nurtured and cherished this one in order for you to have him die like his brothers, to go mad like his father, or to become English like you. I am keeping him with me. Come and get him if you dare."

Yolande might well have afforded to give such an impertinent reply to Queen Isabeau. She felt secure behind the impregnable walls of her château of **Angers**.

Such was the woman, who stood beside the young Dauphin, who surrounded him with the best advisers and who provided him with financial resources.

Back in Paris, Queen Isabeau summoned her son again, but he didn't obey her. He proclaimed himself Regent and led the Armagnacs against their rivals.

In June 1419 Yolande managed to gain an audience with King Charles VI and obtained from him a decree making his son Charles, the Dauphin, a Lieutenant-General of the kingdom, thus emphasizing his legitimacy and his right to the throne. This also served to remove the Queen from the position of Regent.

But the internal struggles between the rival clans didn't cease. It seemed that a possible reconciliation between them was not to be. In September 1419 Charles was to meet the Duke of Burgundy at the Montereau Bridge. That was where the Duke met his end. The war between the two clans was far from finished. And the English still held Paris.

The Queen had long decided that her interests lay with the English King and her allies from Burgundy. The marriage between King Henry V of England and her daughter Catherine of France was celebrated in Paris and Charles VI of France and his Queen Isabeau of Bavaria accepted the English King for their son and successor (Treaty of Troyes 1420). The Duke of Bedford was pronounced a Regent.

The rumours, that the Dauphin was not the son of Charles the Mad, continued to circulate more and more, obviously with the aim to reinforce the position of King Henry V of

England. If Charles, the exiled Duke of Touraine, nicknamed "the little King of Bourges" was a bastard that meant that there was no legitimate heir to King Charles VI, the Mad, and no more obstacles for the son-in-law to the French throne.

It was at about this time, when Jean, the Bastard of Orleans, who was to become known later as Count Dunois, joined forces with "the little King of Bourges". He had been held captive by the Burgundians for a couple of years and had just been ransomed off by his half brother Philippe of Orleans shortly before the demise of the latter.

His two other half brothers, being both prisoners of war in the English camp, Dunois offered his services to the Dauphin. This was only natural. They were related and were about the same age, they had the same enemies and last but not least, the Dauphin had recently revenged the death of the Duke of Orleans, Jean's father.

The Scots, led by John Stuart, had also joined their side and acted as the Dauphin's bodyguards (*Guarde Ecossaise*) from then on. Charles is known to have founded the Royal Scottish Life-Guard, which was still in existence until the French Revolution, continuing thus an old tradition of alliance between the French and the Scots.

Various battles took place; the army of the Dauphin had certain success. He got married to his fiancée Mary of Anjou in April 1422. In the meantime, Henry V, the King of England died, followed shortly by King Charles VI, the Mad. Henry VI succeeded his father Henry V, but Charles, the Dauphin, was the legitimate heir of the French crown. Neither side was prepared to give up, so there were now two Kings of France…

The war continued, with the inevitable pillaging and violence, that the ordinary folk usually suffered. The notorious *chevauchée* tactics, well known from earlier times, became a frequent occurrence during the 100 Years War. This strategy caused a flight of refugees to the fortified settlements on a big scale. It reduced the productivity of the region, which resulted in a lack of vital supplies, both for the civil population and for the armed forces.

In those times when there was no regular army, most lords would bring their own people with them and would be joined by lots of mercenaries, adventurers and the like, aiming to enrich themselves in the process. Charles would've understood during this time the value of a more dependable military force, for later on he would recruit a proper Royal army, paid for by taxes, levied from his loyal subjects...

Back in 1428 the English, after getting reinforcements, advanced into the Loire valley. They easily captured Meung and **Beaugency** just downstream from Orleans, thus taking under their control the respective bridges over the Loire – a sound strategic manoeuvre, for at the time there were only a few bridges over the river - and then moved to the east of Orleans where they took a couple more fortifications, before finally laying siege to Orleans itself.

Why Orleans? Orleans was an obvious choice; it was one of the most important cities in France, along with Paris and Rouen; located at a very strategic point; taking it would open the way for them to Berry, Bourbonnais, Poitou, which were the core of "the little King of Bourges" territory.

That must've been very frustrating for Jean, the Bastard of Orleans, by then a Lieutenant-General of the Dauphin's forces: after all, Orleans was his father's fiefdom; now by rights it belonged to his half-brother Charles, the present Duke of Orleans, sadly still prisoner of the English...

In October 1428 Charles VII convened in **Chinon** the States General of the central and southern provinces which were still faithful to him. That was the way to replenish his coffers. The Royal finances had been left in the doldrums and at the same time the war against Henry VI, the King of England and Paris had taken a particularly bad turn. Charles needed subsidies to keep him going. The sum of 400 000 *livres* was thus accorded to him to "to resist the English troops who were at the present moment at the riverside of the Loire, to be of service to Orleans and for other affairs of the State."

In the meantime the Bastard of Orleans, together with other nobles and about 1200 men entered the city of Orleans and despite the siege, established communication with their allies from the outside. More troops were joining him until gradually there were about 7000 to defend the city. Yet it seemed that they were fighting a losing battle.

"The Herring Affair" which was the abortive attempt of the defendants of the city to capture a supply of victuals and salt fish destined for the English troops, left them disappointed, but still unyielding.

King Charles meanwhile found the situation so hopeless that he proposed to abandon not just Orleans, but Touraine and Berry. Jean of Orleans argued the point with his Royal cousin, but it became clear that he couldn't rely on reinforcements.

Some diplomacy was needed. So he tried to undermine the alliance of the English with the Burgundians. The Duke of Burgundy, Philippe the Good (*le Bon*) was thus approached and persuaded to take care of the lands belonging to the Duchy of Orleans until the return of the rightful owner, the Duke of Orleans, but in exchange was to keep his neutrality.

Consequently the Duke of Burgundy left the siege after an unsatisfactory exchange with a very arrogant Duke of Bedford. The latter had allegedly remarked that "he would not have bothered beating the bush that another may have the bird". No surprise the Duke of Burgundy was insulted.

The relief of the people of Orleans was short-lived. The English got more reinforcements and increased their efforts.

Jean, the Bastard of Orleans needed a miracle to save the town. And the miracle happened!

Enters Joan of Arc, all the way from Lorraine, she is desperate to fight the English, because she is on a mission. And she comes in the nick of time.

It's all very romantic, I am sure, and very noble and very valiant, but...there is a big question mark here. It's too convenient to be just fortuitous. It is almost as if someone had planned it.

It is not difficult to pinpoint who that might be - Yolande d'Aragon. Her son René had married the heiress of Lorraine, Isabelle, so there was an obvious connection there. And it was Yolande, who had launched Joan of Arc both on the political scene and on the battle field.

Yolande d'Aragon was really on the ball. After the demise of her husband, the Duke of Anjou, she had in her hands the House of Anjou with all the resources it had to offer. She had been up to a variety of manoeuvres and schemes to further her plans: to safeguard the Duchy and to place her favourite son-in-law on the throne.

A chronicler of the House of Anjou writes about her: "She was considered as the wisest and most beautiful Princess of the Christian world."

We may well believe it (her image is depicted on a stained glass window in the Cathedral of Le Mans). Later on her grandson Louis XI would say about her that "she had a man's mind in a woman's body". And yet the pivotal role she played in these events remained somewhat hidden to say the least. Of course she must have intended it that way. In order for her plan to work, she had to remain back stage.

What if a nice, inexperienced, romantic girl of 17, was discovered from a far away province; a maid who was hearing mysterious voices and believed she was the chosen one to save her people from a foreign invader? And what if one of the interested parties decided to make use of her to pursue their goals?

In fact certain historians are convinced that this was the case.

From this distance in time it is impossible to say. We can only speculate whether Joan of Arc was really a clairvoyant, a religious zealot and the dupe of another's ambitious and unscrupulous hands, who found in her the tool they needed to further their plans.

Whatever the truth, Joan of Arc came to **Chinon** in 1429 to meet Charles VII and to proclaim that he was the rightful heir to the throne and would be crowned in Reims, for this was God's will. It was said that she recognised him amidst his 300 courtiers, wearing plain clothes, while one of his men appeared in his full kingly regalia.

The question is why the King would want to confuse the poor girl? Why did he then decide to send her to the court of Poitiers to be questioned again and again by the ecclesiastics? In Poitiers she had to establish a reputation, to remove any doubts about witchcraft, to confirm that her inspiration truly came from God. She had to be accepted as the chosen one, sent by God to deliver her people. This she duly accomplished.

From this point the cause of the Dauphin started to win more and more supporters. By recognising him and pledging allegiance to him, she achieved the first objective – removing the doubts surrounding his birth. By requesting to lead his army, she reached the second objective – by putting the experienced warriors to shame.

The château of **Chinon**, where this famous meeting took place is impressive, outlined against the sky when you look up from the banks of the Vienne River. At the time of Joan of Arc, it was a real fortress. A main Royal residence during the time of Charles VII, he installed his court there as early as 1427, when he was still "the little King of Bourges".

Then Joan of Arc arrived at **Chinon** the following year, all the way from Lorraine, to meet him. This was the turning point, not just of his life, but of the history of France as well…

The château is best seen when coming from the south. Perched above the river, we can clearly distinguish the different parts of the castle that still stand – the *Fort du Coudray* on the left, the massive *Château du Milieu* - in the middle as the name suggests, accessible via the narrowed *Tour de l'Horloge* (the clock tower) which still keeps its roof and machicolations. Fort St. Georges, now demolished, used to be to the right.

The Royal apartments (*Logis Royaux*), which have been recently restored, are situated along the south wall of the *Château de Milieu*.

This is the château, which admitted Joan of Arc, wearing men's clothing, on this fateful day of 1429. From the great hall, situated on the first floor, where the court was then assembled, only the monumental fireplace remains. We have to use our imagination to picture it under the glimmering light of 50 torches, full of gentlemen wearing fine clothing. And then a modest provincial girl appeared in front of this assembly and …changed everything.

The King was hiding amongst his courtiers and someone else was wearing his robes. Yet Joan went straight up to him and addressed him respectfully with the words: "Gentle Dauphin, my name is Joan, the Maid. Our Heavenly King sends me as an envoy to tell you that you will be anointed and crowned at the city of Reims".

Charles did not readily believe her of course, but can we blame him? She was sent first to Poitiers to appear in front of the court there and a board of doctors and matrons had to decide if she was indeed inspired or possessed by evil. Her naivety and her piety and more importantly her swift repartee convinced even the most sceptical theologians of her sincerity and they informed the Dauphin that there was a "favourable presumption" about the divine nature of her mission.

That was enough for Charles. However he was persuaded to put Joan to the test i.e. by sending her to relieve Orleans.

From then on events started to unfold fast. Yolande, the Duchess of Anjou had arranged the financing of an army to go to Orleans.

There could not have been any question of Joan leading the army. Whatever the girl believed, there were never any plans to give her *"carte blanche"*. Some historians are almost indignant at this lack of cooperation on the part of the King.

Far from being the one leading the army, Joan must have been just the "morale officer" as we might say today, the one who was able to convince the combatants that God is on their side. She had a sword, but she never killed anyone with it, at least that's what she affirmed later at her trial.

She had her own standard; in fact historians say that there were three ensigns (flags with special insignia), that she used, because that was the practice of the day. The Treasurer of Charles VII paid an artist in Tours to create a Battle Standard (a long triangular flag ending with two tails) and a Pennon (a smaller triangular standard); there was also a religious banner to call the combatants to prayer.

Various contradicting testimonies have come down to us as to the image on her standard; it seems that it represented the Lord with an angel on each side on a white background with golden lilies and *"Jhesus Maria"* written on it. It's possible that the Pennon might have been different from the Standard, with the image of the Virgin and representing the Annunciation. In any case they must have been unusual in some way, because they attracted attention.

People gathered courage from being under her standard, drawn by the innocence of that child. They believed that she was indeed under Divine protection.

Joan was victorious - till her sad fate at Compiegne, her trials and her martyrdom in Rouan.

But at first it all went surprisingly well. Jean, the Bastard of Orleans organised and facilitated her initiation in battle, where she was accompanied by a motley crew, including amongst others, Gilles de Rais (who was to gain notoriety at a later stage), Etienne de Vignolles (nicknamed *La Hire* - Anger, for his cruelty), Louis d'Amboise (who would later lock his wife in his château Talmont) and with great enthusiasm and all, Orleans was finally delivered in May 1429. This won Joan the name "The Maid of Orleans".

Now there was no stopping her. In the beginning of June she went all the way to the Royal city of **Loches**, accompanied by Jean, the Bastard of Orleans, Gilles de Rais and some others to persuade the King, who was there at the time, to go to deliver Reims in order to be consecrated!

The grand château at **Loches** still remembers this fateful meeting. In the great hall (named later after the heroine), where the audience took place, a tile in the floor indicates that important date. At that time this space was twice as big; the present ceiling didn't exist. Today, apart from tapestries, wooden benches and armaments from the 15th century, there is a glass case, displaying a copy of the manuscript of the process against Joan of Arc in 1431.

"Noble Dauphin," she pleaded back there in 1429, "please, do not persist with all those councils, so numerous and so lengthy, just come as quickly as possible to Reims to take the crown, which is yours by right!"

She was very persuasive. To Reims they were destined to go then.

On the way the Royal army gave battle and won a victory at Patay, near Orleans.

In July 1429 Charles VII reached Reims, which opened its gates to him and he was consecrated by the Archbishop Renault of Chartres in the Cathedral St Remi. Joan, the Maid of Orleans stood beside him throughout the ceremony, holding her standard.

So far, so good. But from that moment on, the King and the Maid went on two divergent paths. The King wanted to proceed cautiously, using diplomacy, while the Maid, encouraged by her success, wanted to carry on and expulse the English from the country.

There were a lot of intrigues going on at court and Joan was either unaware of them, or not in the slightest interested to get involved, for she had other priorities. The court was like a minefield. There were camps, there were alliances formed and dissolved as interests shifted.

There was for one the Supreme Commander of the French armies, Richemont, later Duke of Brittany, who was out of favour with the King. Joan had tried in vain to reconcile the two men. Then there was a rivalry between the House of Amboise and the House of La Tremouille that had started in 1428 and where things were escalating to boiling point.

La Tremouille had become a favourite of the King and his Chamberlain. He had ousted the Supreme Commander Richemont, who had introduced him to the King in the first place. Louis d'Amboise with a few others from the Richemont camp, had tried, but failed, to kidnap him in the beginning of 1429. Presumably La Tremoille, who had loads of informants, had smelled "a rat".

Louis d'Amboise had fought alongside Joan of Arc at Orleans, but so had Gilles de Rais, one of La Tremouille allies.

No doubt the Maid must have felt out of place in that court with its shifting sands no less hazardous than the sands of the Loire itself. The King tried in vain to appease her. He gave her a title and kept her close to him.

But the Maid was not able to stand still while she considered her work unfinished. She dashed to Paris to continue her fight. Such behaviour was becoming inconvenient for many, to say the least. Joan had played her role and very well too, but it was not wise to leave her at large.

The Maid might well wonder why she was left to her fate and why no one came to her rescue. Obviously no one wanted her to be rescued. Joan of Arc would serve them a lot better dead, than alive.

She had gained enormous popularity by that time, but a prophetess, who claimed to hear divine voices, telling her what to do, was not going to listen to mere mortals, no matter were they kings or priests. Because of her fame and her large following, the girl had become a loose cannon and presented a danger not just to the English, but also to the French establishment and the Catholic Church.

From this it becomes obvious that nothing was as clear cut in the chain of events that followed, as we have been led to believe. First abandoned, Joan of Arc was captured by the Burgundians, sold to the English, then tried and executed, only to be rehabilitated later by King Charles, beatified and finally made a saint in the 20th century.

She was burned at the stake on the 31st May 1431. Meanwhile the King had new problems to deal with. Just a few weeks earlier, on the 8th of May, another trial had taken place in Poitiers. Louis d'Amboise, together with two accomplices, was charged with the attempted kidnapping of the monarch himself and sentenced to death.

In fact the conspirators had decided to put the plan of 1429 back on the agenda; to kidnap (even kill if necessary) La Tremoille and take the King to **Amboise** to put pressure on him and have him reinstate the Great Council to include people from the Richemont camp. They intended to put it into action while attending a hunting party to which they had been invited by the King. The plan backfired; the conspirators were arrested and imprisoned. The two accomplices were duly executed, but Louis d'Amboise was spared (it seems at the bidding of La Tremoille).

Later on (1434), his cousin Pierre d'Amboise, with a few others, did manage to kidnap the unfortunate La Trémoille. They locked him in the château of **Montrésor** and kept him there till they received a ransom and a promise to liberate Louis d'Amboise, which was done some time later.

The château of **Amboise** (amongst many others) actually belonged to Louis d'Amboise, but was confiscated by the King, as punishment for his actions. The King was to sanction the proposed marriages of his daughters.

As he didn't have a son and heir, Louis d'Amboise was preoccupied with those marriages. La Tremoille had been very hopeful to obtain the hand of the eldest one, Françoise, for his son (no doubt with an eye to the substantial dowry that went with it). But Françoise was married off to Pierre of Brittany, the future Duke of Brittany.

This same Louis d'Amboise was said to have mistreated his first wife Louise-Marie de Rieux and had her locked in his château Talmont. Their daughters stepped in to defend her. The matter reached the ear of the King himself (Louis XI, the son of Charles VII) who used the situation to appropriate more of Louis d'Amboise's property.

After the death of Louise-Marie de Rieux in 1466, Louis d'Amboise married Nicole Chambes, the daughter of Jean de Chambes, the Lord of Montsoreau. Louis d'Amboise saw also to the marriage of his younger daughter Marguerite, to Louis, the son of La Tremoille, before dying in 1469. His second wife died in 1471. She had become the mistress of Charles of France, the Duke of Berry, and had a couple of children with him.

Jean, the Bastard of Orleans was given the title Great Chamberlain and made a permanent member of the Royal Council in 1436. He joined Richemont, the Supreme Commander of the French armies, to deliver Paris. In 1441 Jean received the title Count of Dunois. **Châteaudun** in the Loire country was given to him by his brother, the Duke of Orleans, and it became his main residence.

After the 100 Years War, where he distinguished himself even further, Dunois extended **Châteaudun**, building an additional wing in the 1460s in the true gothic style, but softened somewhat with the addition of some Renaissance touches, aiming more for comfort than warfare, ideas that were coming from Italy and starting to flourish at the end of the 100 years war. He outlived Charles VII and died peacefully in 1468.

Gilles de Rais, who was appointed Marshal of France at the time of the coronation, retired to his lands in the Loire valley. He organised lavish re-enactments in Orleans *(le Mystère du siège d'Orléans),* commemorating the deeds of the Maid, spending a fortune on actors and costumes.

Afterwards he allegedly dabbled in alchemy and gave himself to debauchery of various kinds leading to his ruin. Notwithstanding his piety, his behaviour brought the wrath of the Church down on him.

It was said that while his fabulous riches were dwindling, he practised witchcraft in the vain hope of regaining them. But worst was his penchant for paedophilia, which led him to some despicable crimes, involving hundreds of children, whom he tortured and murdered.

Arrested for entering a church armed to settle a score with a man of the cloth, concerning a property Gilles de Rais had sold to him, the one-time war hero was subsequently tried for witchcraft, murder and sodomy, finally being sentenced to death.

Even in those feudal times when human life was held cheap, especially that of the poor, whose lives were effectively the property of their overlords, what was revealed during de Rais' trial, was deemed shocking.

Gilles de Rais was hanged and then burned in 1440 in Nantes. As he had shown repentance before his death, his wish to be buried in the church was granted. He was buried in the monastery at De Carmes, which was destroyed during the French revolution.

Later on, Charles Perrault, the well known writer of fables, became so fascinated by this Jekyll and Hyde character, that he immortalised him in his story about Bluebeard. And yet to this day his guilt is questioned, and later historians claim that he was a victim of the Inquisition.

In 1992 the whole affair was examined again by the Senate and Gilles de Rais was (you won't believe this!) posthumously acquitted. But we shall never know the truth about this enigmatic man.

Yolande d'Aragon died in 1442 in **Saumur**. Her son René, known as Good King René (*le Bon roi René*) succeeded her.

It would take Charles VII another 10 years to consolidate his kingdom. More battles, more scheming, but in the end, time did work for him. It's not for nothing that he was called Charles the Victorious (*Le Victorieux*), but perhaps more appropriately, he was also known as Charles the well served (*Le Bien Servi*).

CHAPTER 2

The Beauty and the Beast
(15th century)

Loches. When we refer to the château of **Loches**, we have to make it clear that inside the fortifications there is a complex of buildings, dating from different periods. The keep is from the time of Foulque Nerra, the enthusiastic 11th century fortress-builder, who had it constructed to defend the fortified town from the south, its only vulnerable side. It is an impressive square structure, flanked by the towers *Ronde* (Round) and *Martelet* (Little Hammer), both erected in the 15th century. The *Ronde* was in fact another keep and is also known as the Louis XI tower. There is a torture chamber and several rooms one above the other. But it was the *Martelet* that was notorious for having the most impressive of dungeons, occupying several floors below ground.

    The Royal residence on the other hand, is situated at the opposite end of the fortress and consists of the so called *Vieux Logis,* (14th century) and the *Nouveau Logis,* added during the time of Charles VIII and Louis XII. From the terrace, which offers a fine panorama towards the Indre River and the town itself, one can clearly see the difference in style – the old, which is heavily fortified with four turrets, is in sharp contrast to the new one (15th century), built in the more flamboyant Renaissance style. There is also a 13th century tower which has been known since the 16th century as the Beautiful Agnes Tower.

Agnes was indeed beautiful, her contemporaries were unanimous about that and we can judge for ourselves by her portraits. The masterpiece of the renowned Early Renaissance painter Jean Fouquet is in fact the Melun Diptych, where Agnes is depicted on the right wing as a rather disdainful Madonna with child, sitting on a throne, sporting a crown and a resplendent tight-fitting gown with an ermine cape; the gown reveals her slender figure and one of her white round breasts is exposed.

Peeping out behind her a few solemn looking red and blue-coloured cupid/angels, contrast with the pale figures of mother and child. This somewhat erotic painting looks rather avant-garde in a galleria of the more sombre portraits of her contemporaries. The original is in the Royal Museum for Fine Arts in Antwerp, but there is a copy in the Royal Residence in **Loches**, dedicated to her memory.

She was a lady of honour to the Duchess Isabelle de Lorraine, sister-in-law of the Queen, Marie d'Anjou. King Charles fell head over heels in love with this girl, half his age. The King was not a man with a reputation for chasing after skirts. He was fond of his Queen, who he'd known since they were kids and with whom he had a lot of children. But it is doubtful whether he knew real passion, before he met Agnes.

Hitherto brooding and despondent, Charles became lively and jovial, influenced by this attractive, bright girl and her irresistible *joie de vivre*. Confidant and sure of herself, Agnes became the first lady at court, outshining the rest.

Desirous to please, she set fashions, which everybody followed, spending a fortune on materials; aiming to show her figure to advantage, she introduced the long trained gown, but to make up for it, she went for a big cleavage, exposing the breasts; "opened in front so one could see the tits", according to the Chancellor.

The Queen didn't stand a chance. Unlike her mother, Yolande of Aragon, she hadn't been attractive, even in her prime and besides numerous childbirths had taken their toll; she wasn't vivacious either. The chroniclers of the time note that "her face would scare even the English". Mary of Anjou remained a Queen in name only. Agnes set the trend as the official Royal mistress.

Charles himself didn't have a taste for luxuries, but was only too happy to lavish expensive gifts on his mistress. He bestowed a château on her at Beauté-sur-Marne, just outside Paris, giving him the opportunity to pay her the ultimate compliment, saying: "You are twice my Lady of Beauty" (*Dame de Beauté*). He also gave her the château at **Loches**, the same one where, years earlier, Joan of Arc had come, to persuade Charles to go to Reims and be crowned.

That château came in handy some time later, when Agnes was forced to flee the court. It was Louis, the Dauphin, who threatened her. In the beginning Louis did his best to put up with his father's mistress, hoping perhaps that the relationship would not last. Finally one day he snapped and pursued her, they say, with a naked sword in his hand, till she found refuge in the bed of the King himself. This story reached even the ears of the Pope himself (Pius II).

Charles didn't appreciate that. The Dauphin, now out of favour, was sent to *Dauphiné* (a province whose capital is Grenoble, reserved for the heir to the throne), while Agnes retired to her château at **Loches**. A tower of the château is named after her, though that particular tower was built a lot earlier.

The fortress of **Loches**, towering above the rest of the town, is, as we have said, quite extensive. The Royal residence was built apart and has undoubtedly a Renaissance feel about it. At the time of Agnes it would've been *le dernier cri*. The older part, dating from the 14th century, is more austere with its four towers and a covered way to connect them, but the newer part, dating from the 15th century is realised in the contemporary gothic style.

Next to the Royal residence is the former collegiate church of St. Ours. This is the church that Agnes had set her heart on as being her final resting place. She made her wishes known and bestowed lavish gifts on the church, as if she felt that the end was near.

Encouraged by Agnes, the King had gone to the north on a campaign that was supposed to expulse the English for good, while Agnes was left languishing on her own in **Loches**, heavily pregnant with a fourth child from her Royal lover. On a cold day in midwinter 1450 she decided to go after him, either to caution him of a possible danger or following a premonition of her untimely demise. Agnes died at Jumièges, near Rouen after giving birth to a premature, still born child.

It is said that her last words were: "There are a few things, foul and filthy, of our own fragility." Was Agnes referring to the affliction which caused her death? She was not yet thirty. She didn't live to see the English expulsed from Normandy a few months later.

Her death was so sudden that rumours about poisoning started to circulate. Nothing was ever proved; in more recent times tests were conducted on her remains to find out for certain what had happened to her; traces of toxins (mercury) were discovered, but it still remains a mystery whether this was done with a criminal intent or not, because in those times mercury was used to treat parasitic infections (Agnes was apparently suffering from tapeworm infestation) and was also given to pregnant women.

Distraught, Charles ordered two lavish tombs for Agnes: her heart was buried in Jumièges, her body – at **Loches**, according to her wish. He didn't remain inconsolable forever though; a replacement was quickly found in the person of Agnes' cousin, Antoinette de Maignelais.

But Agnes's story doesn't finish there. After the death of Charles, some eleven years later, the canons from the church of St. Ours decided that they could not tolerate anymore the tomb of such a sinner in their holy grounds; therefore they requested permission from the new King Louis XI to move her remains to the castle. The King said that he did not object, but on the proviso that the gifts Agnes had bestowed would also be given back. The canons on second thoughts determined that she was not such a big sinner after all and deemed it appropriate to respect her last wish.

However in 1777 their successors succeeded to persuade Louis XVI that the presence of her tomb in the chancel of the church got in the way of the religious services, so it was moved to the nave. During the revolution, the tomb was profaned and her remains were placed in an urn and moved to the Royal Residence. In 1970 her splendid tomb with her recumbent statue, made of alabaster, was installed in one of the halls of the château and her remains were placed there too. Finally in 2005 the tomb was reintegrated in St. Ours and that is where she rests today.

Charles VII and Agnes had three daughters, all of them recognised by their father. They were brought up according to their rank and were married off to gentlemen. The second one, Charlotte de Valois was married to Jacques de Brezé. Her husband murdered her after catching her *in flagrante* with his Master of the Hunt. For this he was sent to prison. The only son of the couple, Louis de Brezé succeeded them and later married the famous Diane de Poitiers – the Ever Beautiful, who was to become a Royal mistress herself after his death.

The second daughter of the couple Louis – Diane, Louise de Brezé, will leave lots of descendants from her marriage to Duke Aumale, and they will found Royal Houses all over Europe – Spain, Italy, England, Romania, Bulgaria…

The final battle of the 100 Years War is considered to be the battle of Castillon (now Gironde), fought in 1453 when the English, who had other troubles at home with the War of the Roses about to start, were finally expulsed from Guyenne (Aquitaine), the province that had been theirs for about 300 years, the opulent dowry of Eleanor of Aquitaine.

CHAPTER 3

The Bourgeois Gentleman
(15th century)

Plessis-lès-Tours, situated in La Riche, Tours, in the Loire valley, was the favourite residence of Louis XI, the place where he retired and finally died. When in 1468 the King decided to base himself in Touraine, making Tours so to speak, his capital, he bought the manor house Montils-lès-Tours and built a château in its place, which became known as **Plessis-lès-Tours**. At the time, the château consisted of three wings, forming a U-shape, but only one wing now remains; a Renaissance building in the typical flamboyant style, made of brick and stone, it ends to the west with a staircase-tower. If you are curious enough and find this now forgotten château (which is as much of a challenge as the fairy tale account of trying to discover the castle of Sleeping Beauty), walk along the high fence and you might catch glimpses of the only wing that still stands, a forlorn Renaissance façade which clearly has seen better days.

On the demise of Charles VII, his son succeeded under the name of Louis XI the Prudent (*Le Prudent*), but his cunning diplomatic manoeuvres won him the nickname "universal spider", because of the way he was entangling his adversaries in his webs.

He spent his childhood at **Loches** and was married young to Marguerite of Scotland (he was 13, she was 11). He didn't make her happy and she died 10 years later, lamenting: "Life! Fie upon it! I don't want it mentioned again!"

Born in 1423 during the 100 Years War, Louis had an uncertain childhood, his father fighting countless battles with the English and having various troubles with the Burgundians. By the end of Louis' reign, the English held only Calais; whereas Burgundy, Picardy, Maine, Anjou and Provence had all become part of his fiefdom and the powerful lords from the time of his father had been forced, one way or another, to accept the King as their sovereign.

And yet Louis XI is not remembered as a good monarch. He was far from good looking. He was frugal, even miserly. He was deceitful, sometimes cruel. He didn't even get on with his father.

In 1440 he joined the *Pragerie*, a revolt led by a group of disgruntled noblemen, including Dunois, against Charles VII. The revolt was unsuccessful, but the Dauphin made up with his father and they resumed their battles against the English and the Burgundians.

After a campaign in Armagnac, in an effort at reconciliation with the entourage of his father, he offered 6 valuable tapestries to the Royal mistress Agnes Sorel. All six represented the story of the chaste Suzanne. That was a nice gesture, although not without some innuendo…

But he didn't remain on good terms with that lady; he confronted her again, much to the annoyance of his father. On the evidence of the report of a Papal nuncio "the Dauphin was chasing the Royal mistress with a sword in his hand, seeking revenge for the injury caused to his mother".

In 1451 he arranged to marry Charlotte of Savoy without his father's consent. Fearing the anger of Charles VII, the couple found refuge with the Duke of Burgundy.

It's no surprise then, that the Dauphin met the demise of his father with indifference, if not with joy. He didn't even bother to attend the funeral at St. Denis (just outside Paris, the final resting place of the French Royals).

Louis XI was consecrated in Reims 3 weeks later and then entered Paris; however he didn't remain there long, but came back to the Loire and held court in his favourite château **Plessis-lès-Tours** in Tours.

His wife, Queen Charlotte was installed in the château of **Amboise**, an impressive residence, overlooking the Loire, but he rarely stayed there himself. The Queen did not share the life of her Royal husband and the couple seldom appeared together in public. "She wasn't one of those from which one can derive any great pleasure, but never the less she remained a really good lady," notes Philippe de Commynes, councillor of Louis XI.

Charlotte, "the poor Queen who lacked sparkle" ("*la pauvre reine sans éclat*") wasn't a beauty, but on the other hand she was pious, good natured and very loyal to her husband.

The Queen had a modest life style at **Amboise**; her court consisted of fifteen ladies in waiting, twelve women of the bedchamber, no more than 32 officers; that is persons in charge of various functions like the doctor, the librarian, the chaplain, the lute-player, saddler etc and for her rare outings, she had just 2 carriages at her disposal and an escort of about a dozen cavaliers. However she read extensively, mainly works of piety and morality, and did a lot of charitable work.

The new King in the meantime, set himself to work. He dismissed his father's councillors and appointed his trusted yes-men, mainly from bourgeois stock. He raised the taxes of the rich, discharged the pope's tax-collectors and took control of the ecclesiastic revenues.

Louis XI took advantage of any dynastic strife or opportunity to gain lands or influence.

He was quick to arrange a marriage for one of his daughters, Jeanne, who was born lame and disfigured (a fact that he kept in secret for some time). So he decided on marrying her off to young Louis of Orleans when the two were still infants and thus did not have a say in the matter. Louis was the nephew of Dunois, son of his brother Charles, the poet, who spent long years in England as a prisoner of war. After the demise of his father, the boy was under the tutelage of Louis XI.

He was also the godson of the King and apparently during his baptismal ceremony, which was held at the chapel of the château of **Blois** in June 1462, he had wet the sleeve of his godfather, who especially for the occasion had changed his usual everyday fustian garb for a crimson satin robe with sable furs. "Is this a bad sign?" the King, rather concerned, asked the mother of the boy afterwards. His premonitions seemed to be confirmed when he then lost his balance and almost fell, catching his spur in the covers of the bed where she was resting.

At the time Louis XI still did not have a male heir, and that upset him a great deal. The fact that he should consider such a match clearly illustrates the workings of a crafty mind. On the face of it, it was a fitting marriage – between a Prince of Royal blood and a daughter of the King, so nobody could object on that score. But considering the condition of the bride, the King obviously had hoped that the couple would not have any offspring, which would end that branch of the Dynasty and eliminate any chance for Louis, Duke of Orleans, next in line to the throne.

At the time of the wedding, Louis XI, a cynic at heart actually mentioned it to one of his confidants: "It seems to me that any children that they might have together, wouldn't cost that much to feed…" Jeanne of France was most certainly sterile, but the plans of her father didn't quite work the way he had anticipated, as we shall see later in this story. Ah, the best laid plans of mice and men so oft go awry!

In the meantime Louis XI had to deal with the so called League for Public Weal (*Ligue de Bien Public*). Not unlike the *Pragerie*, that he himself had been involved in during his father's time, this league was now led by Charles, Count of Charolais, son of the Duke of Burgundy, Philippe the Good (*le Bon*) and was intended to defend the interests of the noblemen, whose power had been much curbed by the regime of the new King. The youngest brother of the latter,

Charles, Duke of Berry was also part of it and so was the Count of Dunois. The leaguers eventually had to agree terms with the King.

Throughout his reign, Louis XI was kept busy; what with the English still quick to ally themselves with the Burgundians; the Bretons manoeuvring towards one or another side in order to protect their independence, while at the same time keeping the rest of the great lords in check. He put a lot of effort into cajoling everyone to where he wanted them to be – i.e. in the position of being his loyal subjects.

To a certain extent his bad reputation is due to the rumours spread by his enemies. Some of these stories are probably very far-fetched, others downright false. But the facts of history are difficult to check from this distance of time! Novelists, writing years later, fascinated by this complex character, have not been kind either, and have attributed all sorts of faults and crimes to him.

Louis XI was just a man of his era. He might have been cruel, he was certainly deceitful, but these were harsh times. In the aftermath of the war, he had had to reorganise his realm.

Louis XI could be seen as the bourgeois King; he mixed mostly with the merchant classes and trusted them more than the powerful lords.

Sir Walter Scott, in his novel *Quentin Durward*, likens his conduct to that of a money-changer of Ghent, rather than a successor of Charlemagne.

Indeed Louis XI didn't have extravagant habits and, apart from hunting, which he loved as much as his predecessors did and his successors would, he had a modest life style and dressed simply. However, following the war and all the armed conflicts he had had with his enemies, his financial situation was probably not that brilliant.

Louis encouraged industry and trade, which had suffered so badly during the war, and that won him the moniker the King of Merchants.

In **Tours**, a great commercial city, he felt in his element. He made friends with the most prominent bourgeois and dined with them frequently.

One of them, a Maître Jean, so the story goes, flattered by this familiarity, gathered courage to ask the King to honour him with a title. This was readily granted, but afterwards Louis XI completely changed his attitude towards him and totally ignored him. The poor man wondered what he'd done to incur the ill graces of the monarch and complained. "Come on, Mr Gentleman," replied the King, "when I invited you to sit at my table, I treated you as the first amongst your peers, but now when you are the last, I will upset the others if I favour you in the same way."

The King used spies, because he would rather buy off somebody than use force. Yet he kept his prisoners in wooden cages and he would have them tortured if necessary.

Cardinal Balue, who allegedly came up with the idea of those cages, survived 11 years, they say, in one of them in the château of **Loches**, when the King discovered that he'd been plotting with Charles the Reckless/the Bold, the new Duke of Burgundy, who had succeeded his father Philippe the Good.

The King was rather superstitious and consulted his astrologers every time he had important business to conduct. There is a famous anecdote, attributed to his astrologer Galeotti. He predicted the King success in his dealings with the Duke of Burgundy, saying that the stars were favourable, but instead Louis XI ended up imprisoned by him and had to sign a peace treaty (*Traité de Péronne*) which wasn't very favourable to France.

Understandably Louis XI was furious with Galeotti and sent for him, having arranged with his Provost Marshal, someone known as Tristan l'Ermite, to do away with the astrologer if at the end of their interview he dismissed him with the words: "There is Heaven above us". If however he told him to "leave in peace", not to let a hair to fall from his head. Tristan l'Ermite listened to the conversation, hidden behind a curtain.

The King asked the astrologer rather sardonically, if he, who could predict the future so well from looking at the stars knew the date when he, Galleoti would die. The astrologer suspecting the real intensions of the King replied that he didn't know exactly the date but it was going to be 3 days before the demise of the King himself. Louis XI was stunned. His smile faded and pressing the hand of his interlocutor he led him towards the door repeating in a loud voice: "Leave in peace."

Louis would settle the score with the Duke of Burgundy some time later. Well, his Swiss allies would do it for him, for they had their own grievances against Charles the Reckless. Louis had already bought off the King of England, Edward IV, brother-in-law of Charles the Reckless; also the French King continued to subsidise both René II, Duke of Lorraine, and the Swiss, who were all fighting the Burgundians. They got the better of the Duke of Burgundy at the battles of Grandson and Morat.

Having ransacked the Burgundian camp and seizing a really rich booty, they later organised a mock fashion show of a sort, parading with the elegant garb of the enemy, after haphazardly cutting it up here and there to get an interesting tattered look, which afterwards became very much in vogue. That's where the idea of the so called "slashed doublet" comes from; slashing the fabric of doublets or gowns to expose the bright colours of the contrasting lining of the garment.

As for the Duke, he lost his life a bit later fighting the Lorrainers and the Swiss at Nancy (in the Lorraine) and this left nobody to oppose Louis getting his hands on the Duchy of Burgundy.

The King was not very fond of his close relatives either. There were even rumours that he poisoned his brother Charles (who had taken part in a coalition against him) and his mistress, the widow of Louis d'Amboise, to get rid of them, but this is doubtful; it's more likely that the lovers both suffered from a venereal disease, syphilis, and that it was this that sent them to the grave before their time.

And then there is the way the King dealt with his uncle René d'Anjou. The two men couldn't be more different. The son of Yolande d'Aragon, known as Good King René *(Le bon Roi René),* was a courteous, generous man with an excellent education and taste for the arts, architecture, poetry, tournaments, hunting.

He would've preferred to be a painter or a poet, but the death of his elder brother placed the Ducal crown on his head, together with all the responsibilities for the Duchy of Anjou and for the rest of his domain. René was also the King of Naples and Sicily, but his campaigns in Italy ended disastrously. Chivalrous he might've been, courageous and diplomatic too, but he didn't have a taste for warfare. Strategy was not one of his strong points and he messed things up. But that is with hindsight.

René was based in **Angers**, his birth place, but spent a lot of time in his lands in Provence. His first wife Isabelle of Lorraine died and he handed down the Duchy of Lorraine to their son Jean.

At the age of 44 Good King René married the 21 year old Jeanne de Laval with whom he was in love and she became known as Good Queen Jeanne (*La bonne Reine Jeanne*). He composed in her honour *Le poème Regnauld et Jeanneton.* The couple shared the same passion for arts and culture and they might have lived happily ever after, as they say, in the

Loire valley as in Provence, but nothing is ever perfect and the last years of René's life were marked by a series of disasters.

After first losing his son and heir and then his grandson, both of whom died young, René was to suffer yet other losses. Louis XI had all along had an eye on his uncle's Duchy and decided to make a move now, when the coast was clear.

The King arrived at the château of **Angers** with his army and announced he was coming to visit his uncle, who at that moment was at his hunting residence at Baugé. The Duke promptly returned to Angers to meet his nephew, only to be told to hand him the keys to the city. Stunned by this turn of events the Duke complied and the King placed his garrison there.

Good King René was forced to retire to his lands in Provence, because he didn't want to wage a war with his nephew.

But other storms were brewing on the horizon, well, over the Channel in fact, and then it was that yet another disaster really struck. René's daughter Marguerite d'Anjou was married to King Henry VI of England. The War of the Roses raging, events turned against the Lancastrians and Marguerite was imprisoned in the Tower of London by the York faction, while both her husband and her son were killed.

Her cousin, Louis XI of France, negotiated her liberation, after making sure she renounced her rights to the Duchy of Anjou. Marguerite d'Anjou found refuge with her father René in Aix-en-Provence and stayed with him till the end of his life. She outlived him by only two years, which she spent in her manor in Dampierre-sur-Loire in the Loire valley.

After his death in 1480, René's wife Jeanne arranged for him to be buried in the cathedral of **Angers**, in the tomb he had built, in accordance with his wishes. She had to move the body in secret, hidden in a barrel, because the local people, who wanted their good King to be buried in Provence, would have prevented her.

Louis XI, sadly for him, didn't have such popularity with his subjects. Probably he would have liked to be remembered for something else, perhaps for the founding of the French Royal Mail or for the first French chivalric order – the Order of St. Michael (*Ordre de Saint-Michel*), created so as not to be outdone by the Duke of Burgundy, Philip the Good, who had founded the Burgundian Order of the Golden Fleece.

The goal of this order was to confirm the loyalty of the knights to their King. Dedicated to Archangel Michael, it distanced itself from the pagan connotations of the Order of the Golden Fleece, offering instead to each of its members a golden badge with the image of the saint, standing on a rock (*Mont Saint Michel*) while fighting the serpent.

There is something way more important though, for which Louis XI should be remembered: turning France into a state, by adding Burgundy, Anjou, Picardie and Provence and consolidating it into one territory.

With the passing years, the King became more of a hypochondriac. He surrounded himself with medics, apothecaries, clerics; afraid that he would not be cured of the ailments he suffered from or that he might become a victim of those that hadn't yet afflicted him. In fact according to Philippe Commynes, his councillor, "he always thought that he would not pass the age of sixty and for a long time no French King had ever passed that age (that is from the time of Charlemagne)."

Louis spent a lot of money on his health. Donating some vineyards to an abbey, he noted in the documents for this transaction that "the monks are to pray to God and to Our Lady for our welfare, prosperity and health and likewise for the good disposition of our stomach and that neither wines nor meats would be harmful to us and that we would always be well disposed."

He suffered from gout, stomach troubles, skin disorders, but the most painful were his haemorrhoids. We can imagine that he did not have the best of times in his old age. He took prolonged baths, drank herbal remedies, applied a variety of ointments and sought advice from various physicians.

From 1483 on the King didn't leave **Plessis-lès-Tours** anymore and became a virtual recluse. He became quite paranoiac as well; concerned that someone might make an attempt on his life. Louis, who not only had the castle surrounded by high ramparts topped with iron bars and spikes, but also had a troop of bowmen stand guard at all times. He had Tristan l'Ermite arrest passers-by and travellers on the least suspicion and to then execute them without any proof or trial.

Rare animals were brought from far away countries to distract the grumpy old man, musicians arrived with their instruments to play for him, dancers to perform, but nothing would please him and he would dismiss everybody and pine away bored to tears.

Worn out by numerous cerebral haemorrhages, the King prepared for his death, that he undoubtedly feared, as much as he feared conspiracies or an eventual coup d'état. He died at the age of sixty.

His body, contrary to the custom, was taken, not to the crypt of St. Denis in the north of Paris, but to Notre-Dame-de-Cléry in the Loire Valley, for this was his last wish.

CHAPTER 4

France Marries Brittany, Round 1
(15th century)

Amboise is most picturesque when seen from the opposite bank of the Loire or from the bridge. The château, soaring high above the town, has suffered from the vagaries of time but the part that still stands is a reminder of a long and dramatic history.

A fortification existed here since Roman times. Charles VII confiscated the château from the Counts of Amboise (see why under château Montsoreau) and a lot of work was done in the 15th century. This was a golden age for **Amboise**.

The château was constantly under construction. Charles VIII, who was born there, made it his life's work to enlarge and embellish it, following the new Renaissance trends that had inspired him during his Italian pursuits.

It was Charles VIII who built the Chapel St. Hubert there, *Des Logis du Roi et de la Reine* (the apartments for the King and for the Queen) and the two towers known as *Tours des Cavaliers*. He had the upper terrace widened, to hold a larger parterre, enclosed with latticework and pavilions.

Charles VIII was very different from his father, Louis XI. His health, they say, was rather delicate, his frame – frail, his shoulders - stooping; he wasn't very articulate either. And yet on later portraits he doesn't look as ugly as he was rumoured to be. And the label *"benêt"* (simpleton), used by his contemporaries, seems a bit unfair too. He was brought up far from court and wasn't properly educated. But when he ascended to the throne he put in some effort to remedy that. At any rate he found a way to the hearts of his subjects and is referred to today as Charles The Affable or The Courteous (*l'Affable ou le Courtois*).

When Charles inherited the throne in 1483, he was just a boy of 13, so his sister Ann de Beaujeu, 10 years his senior, became Regent, in accordance with the wishes of their late father, who found her highly intelligent. On his death bed he announced that he entrusts the Kingdom "to the least foolish woman in the world" ("*à la moins folle femme du monde*"). Ann de Beaujeu indeed proved to be worthy of his trust.

However her ascent to power didn't please the Orleans branch of the family, so they went to war over it, a war aptly named at a later stage the Mad War (*la Guerre Folle*). The Duke of Brittany, François II, was also involved in the conflict. Amongst others, he joined the Orleanist cause. The fate of Brittany itself was at stake. Unfortunately his traditional allies, the English, were too busy with the War of the Roses and didn't join him.

In 1488, there was a decisive battle between the Breton/Orleanist and French forces; the latter were victorious; the leader of the Orleans Branch, Louis of Orleans was made a prisoner of war and was incarcerated for three years. His resilience and the influence his wife Jeanne had on the King, her brother, and a certain fondness the latter had for him, were probably the main reasons why he didn't lose his life there.

The Duke of Brittany had to accept the Verger Peace Treaty, which greatly curtailed his powers. He was also put under an obligation to seek permission from the French King when marrying off his daughter and heiress. Worn out by all these cares the Duke died soon afterwards leaving no male heir to his Duchy, just a young girl of 11. Brittany at that time was governed according to a *semi-Salic* law – women could inherit only in the case where the male line had died out.

Anne did become a Duchess of Brittany, but the question of her marriage remained a very sensitive diplomatic issue. In order to protect Brittany from being absorbed by France, Anne had to marry accordingly, choosing amongst her numerous suitors the one who would be able to withstand the French threat. During her father's lifetime, there were discussions of various alliances and she was actually promised to Edward, Prince of Wales, but sadly on the accession of his uncle Richard III to the English throne, the boy disappeared and his fate to this day remains unknown.

Another suitable candidate was the powerful Maximilian I of Austria from the house of Habsburg, a widower at the time. Anne had to act quickly, because her Duchy was plunged again into a war with the French. She accepted to marry Maximilian, thus forfeiting on the Verger peace treaty her father had signed with the French, according to which the French King had to sanction her marriage.

Anne was just a little girl, an orphan, who had recently lost her father, her mother having died a couple of years earlier and who had to grow up very quickly and take on her responsibilities. It wasn't going to be easy and many difficulties were about to come her way.

Harassed from all sides, Anne got married by proxy to Maximilian on the 19th November 1490 in Rennes. It was a bizarre affair, this marriage. According to some German custom, after the religious ceremony, Wolfang von Polheim, a representative of the groom, had to introduce his naked right leg into the bed where the bride was laying, alongside her naked left leg, thus indicating a symbolic bond. Apparently the Bretons present found that hilarious.

But the French were not amused. Furious, Charles VIII seized **Nantes**, the capital of Brittany; it was actually Lord Alain d'Albret who delivered the city into his hands, another candidate for Anne's hand and/or Duchy, whose plans were thwarted by this union.

Charles VIII proceeded to lay siege to Rennes, where Anne was. Anne addresses desperate appeals to her husband, but he busies himself with other affairs and ignores the plight of his young bride. The situation becomes untenable and she is forced to sue for peace with Charles.

Charles proposes various other husbands for Anne, but she won't have any of it, saying that she was only going "to marry a King or a son of a King". Charles changed his tactics. He rushed to liberate his cousin Louis, Duke of Orleans, who was still languishing in prison, quickly made up with him and immediately charged him with a mission – to go and ask Anne's hand in marriage on his behalf!

Now the whole affair was becoming rather farcical! Despite his young age Charles himself was, so to speak, already married to young Marguerite of Austria, Maximilian's own daughter. Alright, she was still a child herself and the marriage was not consummated, but never the less it was a marriage, well sort of. This, of course made Anne his mother-in- law! There was no way they could get wed unless their respective marriages were dissolved by the Pope himself! It's not surprising that Anne, scandalised, would refuse such a notion.

But Charles does not give up. He arrives in Rennes and by some means or other he manages to gain access to Anne's quarters. Suddenly she finds herself caught in an unwelcome tête-à-tête with the young King of France and what happens between them, we can only deduce from the follow-up to this momentous interview. Three days later their engagement is announced without their respective marriages having been annulled.

Charles wrote to his sister Ann de Beaujeu: "Madam, you can be satisfied now. I took Rennes and the girl who is within by such means that were desired by me."

All Europe was shocked by such an outrage on the part of the French King.

One night in the beginning of December 1491, Anne arrived at the château of **Langeais**. This château is in fact a solid medieval fortress, rebuilt and fortified by the late King Louis XI to defend Touraine and to keep precisely the Bretons at bay. It is strategically situated overlooking the Loire, on the border between Brittany and the lands of the

French King. The King himself arrived the same night, having come from **Plessis-lès-Tours.**

The marriage was celebrated *en catimini* (on the quiet) at 7:00 o'clock in the morning on the 6 December. Anne was wearing a resplendent gown, made of gold fabric and trimmed with 160 sable skins. She was 14 at the time, Charles - 21. The vows were exchanged in front of Louis of Amboise, bishop of Albi and brother of Georges of Amboise (Cardinal and Counsellor of the future King Louis XII and builder of the château of **Chaumont**). The marriage ceremony was celebrated by Jean of Rély, Bishop of Angers and confessor of Charles.

Ann and Pierre Beaujeu were present, so was Louis, Duke of Orleans, who along with François, Count of Dunois (the son of the Bastard of Orleans), had been instrumental in arranging this marriage. Dunois himself hadn't lived to see the fruition of it, having died just prior to that. Otherwise the wedding party was rather small, but the impact this union had was enormous.

The marriage contract was more like a political treaty, stipulating that the spouses mutually gave each other rights on Brittany, which from that moment on was attached to the French crown. In the case where the monarch died without a male issue, the Queen was to regain the possession of her Duchy, but on the proviso that she should marry his successor, so France could keep Brittany.

The next morning six bourgeois, representatives of Rennes, had to certify that the marriage had been consummated.

The Pope, Innocent VIII, had to annul Anne's marriage to Maximilian a couple of months later (15 February 1492), as if it had never been entered into. Anne was consecrated and crowned in the basilica St. Denis.

We can imagine that Maximilian of Habsburg wasn't at all impressed by this. Anne, his wife, was taken from him, while Marguerite, his daughter was to be sent back. The

French kingdom, more or less encircled by the House of Habsburg, had managed to escape from its predicament and was going from strength to strength.

Maximilian went on to recover Franche-Comté, which was given to France as a dowry for his daughter. Charles left him to it; a treaty was later signed to that effect. Various other treaties were also signed, agreements by which France lost certain territories, but did ensure continuous peace at home till the end of Charles' reign.

Charles was now more interested in Italy; to assert the rights of the House of Anjou he belonged to. Let's not forget he was the descendant of Yolande of Aragon, one time Queen of Naples. However since her time everything had changed. There were other interested parties, notably the Spaniards, and of course there was a King who ruled there.

The Pope had been waging a war against Ferdinand I of Naples, because the ruler of Naples wasn't paying his tribute to the papal state, and eventually decided to excommunicate him. He had then proceeded to invite Charles VIII of France to intervene, proposing to him the Kingdom of Naples. Charles was in an awkward situation at the time, busy dealing with the issues in Brittany.

In the meantime the Pope signed a peace treaty with Ferdinand I. It is doubtful in any case that he really wanted Charles in Naples; most likely he was looking to intimidate Ferdinand with a display of force, showing that he had French backing during the negotiations with him. But the young French King and his retinue took the proposition seriously.

Innocent VIII died shortly after and the new Pope Alexander continued to court the French in the same way, using them as the bogeyman, because in Italy the French "fury" in combat had become legendary. At the same time of course hoping, that they would be too busy with their own affairs, to be able to come. However once the business with Brittany was sorted out, Charles VIII of France was ready for a new challenge. And Italy, being Italy, that is, not a single entity but a cluster of numerous kingdoms and principalities, was a tempting destination to gain glory and lands, being a disunited country with rulers having conflicting interests. There was too no lack of Italian supporters, eager to see Charles enter their homeland. This is how his Italian campaign starts and with it his love affair with the country.

Whatever else might be said about his Italian venture, there is no denying that with it, he opened the door to the Italian Renaissance, which had inspired him. The first signs of it were appearing in France at the time, but it was already in full bloom in Italy, its birthplace. The young King brought home not just objects of art, but a retinue of architects, artists, craftsmen, decorators, gardeners etc and put them to work on the château of **Amboise**.

A fortification had existed at **Amboise** since Roman times. Charles VII confiscated the fortress from the Count of **Amboise** and a lot of work was done on it in the 15th century. Amboise was the site where a garden, laid out somewhat in the Italian manner was to be first seen in France: the origin of the so called French Formal garden.

Charles VIII was born in **Amboise** and wanted to leave his mark. And not just his coat of arms – the blazing sword, a symbol which is so prominent there, together with the fleur-de-lis, the ermine of Brittany and the Franciscan rope (the last two crests come from Anne of Brittany). The medieval fortress was gradually transformed into a magnificent Royal residence.

A garden designer from Naples, named Mercogliano, extended the terrace of the château, surrounded it by galleries, and laid out four parterres around a central pavilion.

Influenced by what he'd seen in Italy, Charles had two massive towers constructed, allowing horsemen and even carriages to proceed from the river bank to the terraces of the château, 40 m high above the Loire. Those towers have survived to this day and visitors can walk up to the higher level along a wide ramp in the form of a spiral – for those times this was a truly revolutionary project!

While Charles was thus occupied, Queen Anne was busy producing children; she was pregnant most of the time – with a child every 14 months on average. Sadly all six of them died in infancy. This didn't leave her much time to concern herself with the affairs of state. During the Italian campaigns, it was Ann de Beaujeu, her sister-in-law, who was mostly involved with them.

The Queen grieved deeply over the loss of her children. She had a lavishly decorated little oratory built especially for her at **Amboise** and she spent a lot of time praying there. Her husband didn't quite know how to console her; he pondered on ways to distract her. At one time he even thought that a game or two of tennis might just do the trick!

In the end it was precisely a game of tennis he was going to see when he hit his head on a lintel, fell back and died a few hours later as a result, at least that's what they say. They also say that two of his servants died as well – of broken hearts. He was only 28.

CHAPTER 5

France Marries Brittany, Round 2
(16th century)

Blois belonged to the Counts of **Blois** from the 10th until the 14th century (only a pointed gable remains from that period, incorporated in the château we see today); the County was acquired by the brother of Charles VI, Louis, Duke of Orleans, at the end of the 14th century; thereafter the court of Orleans was held in **Blois**.

The future Louis XII was born there and an 1857 copy of an equestrian statue of him (the original was destroyed during the revolution) can be seen in an alcove above the gateway of the chateau. Louis looks handsome here, carrying his weapons, wearing his crown and riding a horse, ambling along. Underneath can be seen his crest – the porcupine with a crown and the monograms "L" and "A" on each side.

Having become a Royal residence, the importance of the château increased. A new wing was added, built of brick and stone in the traditional gothic style, but with a hint of Italianate influence in the decorative features. Balconies mark the locations of the apartments of the King and the Queen; the Royals used to watch games and tournaments held in the courtyard just below.

Various other improvements were made to transform **Blois** into a sumptuous Royal palace. The Chapel St. Calais was reconstructed and consecrated in 1508. A gallery, leaning against the chapel connected the new wing with another older wing at the back of the courtyard.

Gardens and terraces were laid (long since disappeared), designed by the Italian master gardener, Pacello, of **Amboise** fame.

Some go as far as to say that the château of **Blois** is an early Renaissance equivalent of Versailles of Louis XIV. However that comparison is superfluous, **Blois** was just not built with the panache and on such a grand scale as Versailles, neither was it as sumptuous as its more renowned later successor.

Nevertheless what we see today is in fact a sort of open air museum, showing the development of architecture over four centuries in joining together around the same courtyard four different periods: Feudal (the States General building and Foix Tower – both from the 13th century); Gothic-Renaissance transitional (Charles d'Orléans Gallery, St. Calais Chapel, Louis XII wing – late 15th – early 16th century); Renaissance (François I Wing, the façade of the Loges – 1515-1524); Classical (Gaston Orleans Wing (17th century).

Louis XII is remembered as the Father of the people (*Père du peuple*) and during his reign the monarchy reaches a stability that it hasn't known for a very long time. According to Machiavelli, who was twice on a mission to France: "the crown and the Kings of France today are stronger, richer and more powerful than ever".

Louis XII was from the Orleans branch of the family (the son of Charles of Orleans, the poet and grandson of Louis, Duke of Orleans, the same who was assassinated by the Duke of Burgundy in 1407) and was married to the late King's sister Jeanne of France. But this match, advantageous at one time, had outlived its usefulness at the moment Louis ascended to the throne.

It wasn't just because Jeanne had been unable to produce an heir; there was also the sensitive issue of Brittany and the marriage contract between Anne and the late King. After the death of her husband, Anne had retired to her Duchy and had taken things into her own hands and of course she had every right to do so.

Whether Louis had been in love with Anne all along, is difficult to say, whatever the rumours might have implied. He had known her since she was little, due to his alliance with her late father. He had been instrumental in her marriage to Charles and was present at their wedding. Even if at that time there had been some attachment between these two ambitious souls, it would've been buried deep down and never given any expression.

However, the political situation had now changed and therefore the road was open for King Louis XII to approach the Duchess and negotiate marriage terms. This time round it was Anne who was in a better position to dictate them. Besides, Louis first had to obtain an annulment of his marriage to Jeanne of France from the Pope.

He claimed that the marriage was never consummated, because of Jeanne's physical disadvantages, something that Jeanne contested vigorously. Ironically Anne, his intended bride, is also said to have been lame. The Pope however did not choose to cause any problems; he took advantage of the situation to obtain from Louis XII, in exchange for the annulment of his marriage, the title Duke of Valentinois for his bastard son César Borgia, brother of the infamous Lucretia Borgia (yes, in those times the popes had bastard children like everybody else and Pope Alexander VI Borgia, notorious for his debauchery, was no exception). César is now also known as Le Valentinois.

Louis XII was at **Chinon**, when a legate of the Pope brought him the bull for his divorce, dated 17 December 1498. It shall come as no surprise that he was overjoyed and had a big celebration.

The unfortunate Jeanne retired to a convent in Bourges and later founded a religious order called Annunciate in honour of the Virgin Mary. She was finally canonised in 1950 by Pope Pius XII.

The marriage with Anne of Brittany was celebrated on the 7th January 1499 in **Nantes**. The new marriage contract was radically different from the one signed at the time with the late Charles VIII. Her new husband acknowledged her rights on Brittany in their entirety in her position as the sole heir of the Duchy and her title Duchess of Brittany. In return, the Royal power was exercised by Louis XII, who took the title Duke - Consort, no matter that the decisions were taken in the name of the Duchess.

After the marriage Anne settled in **Blois**, where symbols of her presence can still be seen today – such as the monograms "L" and "A" for Louis and Anne, above the windows of the Louis XII wing, or her crest – the ermine along with that of the porcupine of Louis. The Royal couple usually spent their winters in this château.

But the King had other fish to fry before he could settle down with his new wife: Italy was waiting for him and off he went on his military campaigns there. First of all he managed to secure Milan, to which he had a rightful claim from his grandmother Valentina Visconti. He imprisoned Ludovico Sforza, the Duke of Milan in the dungeon at **Loches** and kept him there for 8 years.

Visitors today can still see the paintings and inscriptions Ludovico left on the walls of his cell. When he was finally released from the gloomy underground world of his dungeon and emerged out into the sunlight, his joy was so great and the sunshine so bright, that the poor man collapsed and died on the spot.

Louis XII, in the meantime, went on to win a battle that he fought with the Venetians. He also pursued the claim of his cousin and predecessor, Charles, for the kingdom of Naples.

The French presence in Italy was to be short lived though. In spite of the setbacks Louis XII encountered, he remained a popular monarch. Sadly he did not succeed in producing a male heir to the throne.

Two girls were the only surviving children, born from his second marriage, and the question of the succession was once again on the agenda. He is reported to have said: "We are working in vain. That big boy will spoil everything." The "big boy" in question was his successor to be, François d'Angoulême.

Queen Anne had a lot more influence on her new husband than she ever had on her previous one. Her wish was to arrange an advantageous match for her eldest daughter and her eyes turned towards one of the most eligible (to her mind at least) parties in Europe – no less than Charles of Luxembourg (the future Holy Roman Emperor Charles V), grandson of her former (almost) husband, Maximilian of Habsburg!

As we can see, Anne retained the same ambitious streak throughout her entire life. The Duchy of Brittany was a good enough dowry for the French King, and her daughter Claude was going to offer no less a dowry to her intended husband. Anne did not even consider that her subjects might have something to say on the matter.

The King was sick at the time, so he meekly went along with the schemes of the Queen. Once he recovered though, he found that the match was very unpopular amongst his retinue and he decided to put an end to the engagement.

There was another more promising candidate, and accordingly, the King decided on the engagement of his eldest daughter Claude with François d'Angoulême (if you can't beat them, join them, as they say). The Queen was opposed to this match till the very end. It did not take place until after her death eight years later.

Louis did not lose his hope for a son and hurried to remarry, thinking that a young bride might just do the trick. The beautiful English Princess Mary Tudor, sister of Henry VIII was exactly what he wanted and seemed to breathe new life into him. But not for long. Worn-out by his exertions in the bedchamber, the King passed away soon after. The marriage had lasted only 82 days.

CHAPTER 6

The Chivalrous King
(16th century)

François I (also known as the Prince of the Renaissance, the Warrior King and various other sobriquets) was from the Angoulême branch of the Valois dynasty. He was born in Cognac, but spent his childhood in the château **Clos-Lucé** in **Amboise**.

His father, the Count of Angoulême died when he was an infant and he was brought up together with his sister Marguerite by an ambitious mother, Louise of Savoy. They both received an excellent education.

Marguerite later became the Queen of Navarre (the little Kingdom on the south west border of France) after marrying Henri d'Albret, the King of Navarre and was to become the grandmother of the future King Henri IV, the founder of the Bourbon Dynasty.

Chambord – a masterpiece of the early Renaissance era, this château is emblematic of the reign of the great French monarch. Its unmistakable outlines leave a lasting impression, its grand scale inspires awe, the beauty of every detail makes us marvel at the craftsmanship of its builders.

In his fervour the King even wanted to divert the Loire and bring it to the chateau, but the builders were reluctant to undertake such an ambitious project and a smaller river, the Cosson was diverted instead.

The name of the architect is unknown, though there are speculations about the influence of the great Leonardo, who had died just a few months before. The famous double - helix open staircase is attributed to him (it consists of two spirals intertwined, but not connected, allowing two people to go up or down without ever crossing each others' path).

One thing we know for sure – **Chambord** is François' baby, a project he cherished since his return from Italy. Like his predecessors he was determined to leave his mark; he succeeded to outdo his rivals with this fabulous château in the Italian style. This new Renaissance movement suited him to the core; it corresponded to his taste for grandeur and magnificence.

François I didn't spend more than 40 days in his chateau, but he was able to impress his great rival, the Holy Roman Emperor, with it. In the autumn of 1539 he took the Emperor for a ride in the woods and the sudden apparition of this multitude of turrets at the end of the wooded avenue left Charles V speechless.

"I didn't expect that little thing to interest you!" remarked François mischievously. A group of young girls, dressed as Greek deities came forward to meet the sovereigns and strew flowers at their feet.

The visitor, delighted by this reception and impressed by the château, reputedly said: "Chambord is the essence of human industry".

François I, who had chosen the salamander as his emblem together with the motto "*Nutrisco et extinguo*" ("I nourish and I extinguish" – which might be interpreted as "enduring faith which triumphs over the fires of passion") had this symbol put as a decorative element all over **Chambord** together with his initial "F".

François' reign was marked by great progress, not just in the sphere of arts and architecture, but also in science and technology. Since the invention of the printing press in 1440, print had become the leading medium for spreading information, new ideas, innovations. By the end of the 15th century it had been established all over Europe and had enabled the publishing of millions of books (in the sixteen twenties France was publishing about three hundred titles each year) and thus had facilitated the spread of humanism.

Being a Renaissance man, François I has the reputation of being a humanist, although his education could not exactly be called that; let's say that the influences of his mother and tutors during his formative years made him receptive to this new movement.

In any case the new European trends in philosophy and art appeal to him, and he quickly becomes the patron of humanists, poets, musicians.

Leonardo de Vinci is one of those who benefited from the generosity of the King. François admired him greatly and offered him his hospitality. Leonardo spent the last years of his life in close proximity to the Royal château in **Amboise**, at **Clos-Lucé**, the chateau where the King had spent his childhood and where François frequently came to visit him.

The great artist didn't do much painting though, but got involved in various projects, including the design of a château for the Queen-mother at Romorantin-Lanthenay in the Loire valley, another place that François remembered fondly from his childhood. The death of Louise put an end to this project.

These were exciting times not just for France, but for Europe in general. In the wake of the great geographical discoveries, François recognized the importance of the New World, the riches it offered and encouraged its exploration.

France was flourishing and the Loire valley, the centre of the Kingdom, was at its zenith. But not for very long.

François' antagonists happen to be charismatic characters too – on one side the Habsburg Charles V, on the other, the formidable Henry VIII of England. Rivalry between them was inevitable. Regrettably the wars with the former were particularly damaging, not only for France but for the whole of Christendom. They left Europe more divided than ever.

England, due to its location on the periphery of Europe, didn't play that significant a role in 16th century Europe. The Holy Roman Empire on the other hand, was, at the time, a different proposition altogether. François would love to have been elected as an Emperor on the demise of Maximilian I (the first husband - by proxy - of his mother-in-law, Anne of Brittany), but Charles, a grandson of the late Emperor, was in a stronger position.

At the time of Charles' ascendance to the Roman Imperial throne in 1519, apart from Austria, his lands included the so called 17 provinces (Netherlands, Flanders, Artois etc), Spain and its American territories and the Kingdom of Naples.

The face of Europe was quite different then! And the grand players of the time had different priorities altogether. The Emperor's aim to have a Habsburg dominated Europe wasn't as unreasonable as it might at first seem.

François of course didn't cherish the notion. Alliances were formed and then dissolved and the main protagonists were frequently changing their allegiance depending on the circumstances, much as it happens today. But we are not going into detail there.

Ironically, it was precisely Charles V who was to have been the intended son-in-law of Anne of Brittany - she envisaged this union for her daughter Claude, but it was not meant to be. You win some, you lose some, as they say. If Claude had married Charles instead of François, the map of Europe would've been very different and the fortunes of France would have nose-dived as a result. The country would have found itself encircled and intersected by the Habsburg Empire, because Claude's dowry included the Duchy of Brittany, the Counties of Blois, Coucy, Montfort, Étampes, Ast and the rights to the Duchy of Milan.

Whether Claude would have preferred Charles over François, history doesn't say. The young Queen was an unassuming little thing, who dutifully played her role, produced 7 children, the future King Henri II amongst them, and died an untimely death; she was only 24. She gave her name to a small green plum, the greengage, still known as "*la reine Claude*" in France; a rare sort brought from the Orient some time after her demise and planted in the Royal gardens at **Blois**.

Her death didn't upset anybody greatly and various mistresses succeeded each other into the King's heart (and/or bed). He was very popular with the ladies. They just couldn't resist him. Apart from one, Françoise de Foix, Lady Châteaubriant; she managed to hold out for three years or so, but finally succumbed to his charm. She remained his favourite for about 10 years.

François pursued the Italian campaigns of his predecessors. He had gained a new enemy – Charles III, Duke of Bourbon, the Supreme Commander of the French armies, who had been stripped of his lands (the Bourbonais) by the Queen-mother.

Hell hath no fury like a woman scorned, and rumours had it that she had offered her hand to the Duke after he lost his wife Suzanne (granddaughter of Louis XI), but was rejected. She then pursued the claims she had on his lands (as the granddaughter of Charles I of Bourbon) and won the process.

The upshot was that the Duke changed sides and offered his services to the Emperor, Charles V of Habsburg. Setting the Duke against her son was not a clever move on the part of Louise, but a disaster waiting to happen.

Inspired by the deeds of ancient heroes, the King-knight led his troops personally and took part in the battles. As Napoleon regretfully observed later, he was "a very bad general" and after losing a crucial battle at Pavia, was finally captured by the Emperor and ended up a prisoner of war in Madrid, where he spent more than a year, until he signed the Madrid Treaty, making various concessions to the Empire and leaving his two older sons as hostages in his place.. However he had previously arranged with his secretary of State to regard anything signed during his imprisonment as invalid, due to his ill health during that time.

During his captivity, his mother Louise acted as Regent and organised the affairs of the State exceptionally well, negotiating agreements with the English and with the Ottoman Empire so as to make the release of her son possible. His sister Marguerite was also involved in the negotiations with the Emperor Charles V for the liberation of her brother, whom she dearly loved. Marguerite was a brilliant woman – erudite, smart, one of the first women-writers of France. Clément Marot, the poet, who was her valet at one time, described her as: "woman's body, man's heart, angel's head".

Released from captivity, François was met at Bayonne by his mother and her ladies in waiting. One of them was a certain Anne de Pisseleu, an ambitious and calculating young lady. She managed to attract him so much so that soon he was head over heels in love with her.

After returning to France the King renounced the Madrid Treaty. Unfortunately this led to more conflicts and even at one point to a proposed personal duel between Charles V and François I; it never took place however, but things were getting out of hand and something had to be done. There was also the threat from the Ottoman Empire to be considered. Europe had to restore the peace.

Today the peace Treaty of Cambrai (1529) is known as the Ladies' Peace (*La paix des Dames*), because it was signed by Louise of Savoy, the mother of François I, Marguerite of Austria, aunt of Charles V and Mary of Luxembourg in the presence of Cardinal Louis de Bourbon Vendôme. And a year later, in 1530 François I did marry Eleanor of Habsburg, the sister of Charles V as previously agreed. His sons also finally returned from captivity.

Something else changed too after the return of the King. He turned his attention to Paris and spent less and less time in the Loire valley. It was still a favourite place for festivities, celebrations, hunting, but Paris was gradually taking its rightful place as the capital of France. But it wouldn't be until the reign of Henri IV, when this transition would be fully completed.

Meanwhile Lady Châteaubriant, who really loved the King, fought for him tooth and nail with her new rival Anne de Pisseleu for a period of two years; in vain: finally she had to give up and retired from court. Anne became François' mistress and remained in that position till the end of his life. The King callously asked Lady Châteaubriant to return to him the trinkets, all engraved with amorous inscriptions, that he had given her previously. She had them melted down and sent him back gold ingots with the words: "Take these to the King and tell him that because he desires to retract what he'd bestowed on me so generously, I return it to him, handing it back as golden ingots. As for the inscriptions, I have them imprinted and fixed in my thoughts so well, and cherish them so much, that I can't suffer anybody to have them, use them and enjoy them apart from myself."

The King remained on friendly terms with the lady and in 1531 he left Queen Eleanor in **Blois** and Anne de Pisseleu – in Fontainebleau and went to pay her a visit in Châteaubriant. It wasn't purely a social call; he had of course good reasons to do this. Jean de Laval, the cheated husband, was a governor of Châteubriant and he wanted his support in the delicate matter of Brittany. Jean de Laval couldn't do anything else but oblige his King as he always did and after sumptuous festivities held in the monarch's honour, François left never to set eyes again on the beautiful Lady Châteaubriant, who died some time after either by the hand of her revengeful husband or of a broken heart.

But the King had got what he wanted and, in the summer of the same year, François, the Dauphin entered **Nantes** to be crowned as the Duke of Brittany under the name of François III.

That task successfully accomplished, François I turned to other matters. He still had the intention to form some kind of coalition against his old rival Charles V and to find a way to replenish his treasury, whose funds were depleted as a result of his extravagant lifestyle.

He made an alliance with Henry VIII of England; the latter had troubles of his own at the time – he was trying to obtain a divorce from Catherine of Aragon, who happened to be the aunt of Charles V, in order to marry Anne Boleyn; Pope Clément VII under the influence of Charles V, wasn't quick to grant him his divorce.

François tried to persuade the Pope but wasn't successful either. The upshot was a separate Anglican church to suit Henry. Well, the Valois monarchs might have allowed their mistresses to rule the country instead of them, but they would never have attempted anything so drastic and sacrilegious.

But let's return to François. He set his mind on marrying his son Henri of France to the niece of the Pope, Catherine de Medici, just 14 at the time. Catherine had a rich dowry and he hoped to persuade her uncle Pope Clément VII to help him to accomplish his "Italian dream". Sadly, the Pope died soon after the wedding and young Henri ended up married to a teenage girl, who he didn't care for (she reminded him of her uncle) and who for a long time wasn't able to produce any children.

Catherine was clever and intelligent, but it took her time to assert herself in the French court, where her foreign ways were often laughed at. But love her or hate her, she is one of the few French Queens to be so well remembered by history.

Before she acquired her notoriety, she was just a young woman who would read Greek and Latin, show an avid interest in astronomy, and also pursue other pastimes like riding and hunting, something that appealed very much to the King, her father-in-law.

Anne de Pisseleu in the meantime still managed to keep her position as first lady. It wasn't easy. Constancy wasn't one of François strongest sides. But Anne wasn't really enamoured of him, so she let him have his little flings here and there, provided that he came back to her, which he invariably did.

Despite his licentiousness, François was a religious man. Under his sister's influence he had been for some time tolerant towards the new reformist ideas, spreading in France at the time, but after the notorious "affair of the placards" he started reprisals against the Protestants.

It happened overnight in October 1534 when numerous anti-catholic posters simultaneously appeared in public places in Paris, Rouen and in three major cities in the Loire valley: Blois, Tours and Orleans. The King was outraged to find one on the door of his bedchamber in the château of **Amboise**. Now here the Protestants had gone a bit too far and set the scene for prolonged wars of religion that devastated the country.

But François hadn't forgotten Italy. In 1535 on the death of the Duke of Milan, François hastened to assert his claims on the Duchy. Ultimately this led to nothing, In the meantime young François, the Dauphin died suddenly, and Catherine de Medici found herself the wife of the new Dauphin Henri and a focus of renewed attention.

At seventeen Catherine wasn't particularly pretty, she had a moonlike face, big lips and penetrating, but somewhat bulging eyes. She had attractive ankles though and she knew it. So, in order to display this attribute, she had decided on an audacious way to mount her horse and she is credited with the introduction of the two-horn side-saddle in France. This second horn made all the difference, it held the right leg of the lady-rider allowing her for the first time to face forward and to have independent control of her horse and thus to ride at faster gaits.

This novel way of riding certainly attracted the attention of the gentlemen during the hunting parties, but imposed yet another accessory to the lady's riding outfits – the legging or bloomers (that fashion, the knickers, had of course first appeared in Italy). However it caught on very quickly in France, after Catherine was seen wearing it underneath her flapping skirts.

Neither this nor her other accomplishments endeared her to the heart of the Dauphin, who had eyes only for Diane de Poitiers, who was twice his age. Diane was the widow of Louis de Brézé, a grandson of Charles VII and Agnes Sorel. She was 15 at the time of the wedding and he was nearly 40 years older. There were two girls from their union and when he died some years later, Diane sincerely mourned him.

Henri knew her since his childhood for she was involved in his education and he had a high regard for her; who knows – perhaps he might have had a crush on her at that time. The Prince had even started to dress in black and white as if he was also in mourning, to honour Diane, who wore these colours since her husband's demise.

His constancy must have flattered and finally swayed the pretty widow to become his mistress, which in all probability happened in 1538 and continued till the end of his life.

Interestingly it was precisely Diane, who being a distant relative of Catherine's (the maternal grandfather of Catherine was the brother to Diane's paternal grandmother), had championed the idea of Henri's marriage to the young Florentine, no matter that there had been strong opposition to it on the grounds that Catherine was "a daughter of merchants".

An ambiguous relationship had since developed between the two women; although Diane was frequently directing her lover towards his wife's bedroom, and Catherine pretended to accept this *"ménage à trois"*, it wasn't until

Henri's death years later that she was finally able to vent her real feelings towards her husband's mistress.

However at this earlier period, she desperately needed Diane's support because she still hadn't managed to produce an heir and there was the threat of repudiation. Henri wasn't sterile; it was known that he had already had children out of wedlock. And, after spending more time with his wife, it became obvious that Catherine wasn't sterile either and finally, after ten years of marriage, she gave him the offspring so desired by the couple. She was forever pregnant after that, and relieved, Henri, still not particularly bothered with Catherine, was able to devote his time to Diane.

Diane as always was the most important person in his life, a mother figure, a mistress and a confidante, all rolled into one, but he was getting increasingly annoyed with Anne de Pisseleu, who was gaining more and more influence over his father as time went on.

At one time the King even decided to give his mistress a husband as a present, not because he wanted to get rid of her, but in order to give her a rank and bestow a title on her; he chose Jean de Brosse and gave him the title Duke of Étampes and Duke of Chevreuse, so Anne now became Duchess of Étampes.

Diane de Poitiers hated her. There was a bitter rivalry going on between the two women, escalating into the notorious affair of the "*Coup de Jarnac*" which wasn't resolved until the ascendance of Henri II. Both women had their admirers, their fans, their poets, their artists - their coterie in short, but also they had their enemies. According to the shifting allegiances the experienced courtesans had to be quick and evaluate the situation at any given moment or even gauge future developments in order to stay afloat.

Benvenuto Cellini, the famous Italian sculptor, describes in his autobiography his stay in France where he was invited by the King. He did not get on with the Duchess of Étampes though. On completion of his famous statue of Jupiter, commissioned by the King, the Duchess kept François away till the evening either because she hoped that he would not bother to go and see it or because she thought that in the evening, under the artificial light, it would not look so well. However Benvenuto had installed a torch high above it and had employed a little boy to turn the light slowly round so that when the King and his party finally arrived, everybody was greatly impressed by the work of the artist.

Jupiter looked almost alive with thunder in one hand and a globe in the other. Benvenuto had also covered the groin of the statue to spare the ladies the view of the phallus of the god. The Duchess of Étampes, in an attempt to belittle his work, suggested that it was undoubtedly covering some imperfections. Benvenuto then pulled the wrap away to reveal the splendid nudity of the deity. The King praised him but the Duchess was furious. The artist hastened to leave France for he feared reprisals.

In his old age, François I relied more and more on Anne's judgement. However things were going from bad to worse because in her efforts to get rid of her rival Diane, she didn't have any scruples, even prepared to gamble on the Kingdom itself, resorting to treachery and endangering the life of the Dauphin, whom she equally hated. Miraculously he kept out of harm's way, but he might well have wondered why during his military campaigns it appeared that he was forever at the wrong place at the wrong time and that the enemy seemed to know precisely his whereabouts. He must have realised at one point that Anne Pisseleu was to be blamed for that.

All the scheming led to nought and when François, decrepit and disease ridden (not surprisingly syphilis was just one of the afflictions he suffered from), finally died at the age of 59, Anne had to face a life of exile. Diane was not very severe with her for she didn't want to set a precedent, but she did ban her from court. The ex-favourite, stripped of her title, retired to her lands and lived the rest of her days forgotten by all.

    Catherine de Medici did not have a say in the matter. Nobody sought her opinion. With the demise of her father-in-law, with whom she always got on, she had become a Queen, but in name only. It was Diane who called the shots. The uneasy relationship between the two women is explored in the book "The Serpent and the Moon: Two Rivals for the Love of a Renaissance King", recently published. The Princess Michael of Kent, the author of this work is a descendant of them both and therefore of Charles VII of France and Agnes Sorel.

CHAPTER 7

The Rule of the Huntress
(16th century)

Chenonceau. The history of **Chenonceau** is compelling – it's now known as the château of six women and what we see today is indeed the result of the consecutive efforts of these women; each connected with the château at different stages of its existence.

It's situated on the river Cher, a tributary of the Loire. The château started its life as the residence of an upstart financier Thomas Bohier, who came to power at the end of the 15th and beginning of the 16th century, occupying political functions and serving Louis XI, Charles VIII, Louis XII and François I.

His wife Katherine Briçonnet was the one who made **Chenonceau** her life's work, but sadly didn't have time to enjoy it. Her son had to give it up to the crown, because after his father's demise, it became clear that the shrewd man had embezzled funds from his Royal master to finance his project.

This is how **Chenonceau** became a Royal property and passed from the hands of one woman to another, each of them putting their heart into it as if they knew that at some future time, when they would not be around anymore, it would acquire international fame and would be admired by thousands of visitors (it is the most visited château on the Loire, second only to Versailles in the whole of France).

The château is not very big and pleases the eye with its harmonious proportions. The visitor could be forgiven if they overlook the fact that it consists of two, very different, parts.

The Marques tower on the right bank of the river Cher is the oldest one and the only surviving part of the medieval edifice built by the previous owners, the Marques family.

The rest was razed to the ground by Thomas Bohier. It was the keep of the original fortress. To give it a more modern appearance, the new owner installed large mullioned windows in the Renaissance style, hid the embrasures/crenels, added a pinnacle turret and finally had the letters "TBK" (corresponding to Thomas, Bohier and Katherine) sculpted on the façade.

The same letters can also be seen in the main building together with the motto: "*S'il vient a point, me souviendra*". It's not clear what the meaning of this phrase is, but perhaps it is along the lines of: "If it's finished (the château), I will be remembered."

The Renaissance two-storey residence is built on an almost square plan (22 m/23m), flanked by corner turrets and rests on the massive stone blocks of the old mill that was here before.

Henri II was consecrated in Reims in 1547 and the following month he made a solemn entry to **Blois**, accompanied by "naked women, riding oxen", presumably to evoke the Greek myth about the abduction of Europa by Zeus in the guise of a bull. That scandalized a lot of people. A big tournament was then organised in the château to celebrate the event.

One of the first matters that Henri II wanted sorted out after he succeeded his father, was the affair of the "*Coup de Jarnac*", that François had wanted forgotten. It concerned a certain Guy Chabot, later Baron de Jarnac, who had married Louise de Pisseleu, Anne's sister. Henri, at that time the Dauphin, at his mistress' instigation started a rumour about an alleged affair between the young man and his step-mother, Magdelaine de Puyguyon.

Outraged Anne de Pisseleu, by that time the Duchess of Étampes, demanded her lover to act. The Dauphin, who feared his father's anger didn't dare to admit anything, so it was a friend of his, La Châtaigneraie, a great swashbuckler, who took it upon himself to declare that it was he who started the rumour, repeating what young Chabot had said himself. Chabot asked the King's permission to defend his honour, but the King refused, only too aware that all was a result of the jealousy between women. Besides he had a high regard for both men concerned and he didn't want them embroiled in such an affair.

Now with the ascent of Henri II to the throne the situation changed completely for Chabot, by then Baron de Jarnac. Related by marriage to the ex-favourite automatically put him out of favour, so he approached the King with the same plea. This time he was given the opportunity to prove his worth and the delay was actually to his advantage because he had used it wisely to take a lot of lessons in fencing and had learned a trick or two. It was also fortunate for him that he had not wasted his time for the duel took place in front of a big crowd, the King and Diane de Poitiers being amongst the audience too.

His opponent La Châtaigneraie was athletic and robust, while Jarnac was slim and lithe. At the beginning of the duel it seemed that Jarnac didn't stand a chance; then suddenly he took his opportunity: lurched forward and pierced La Châtaigneraie behind the knee, cutting the ligament and bringing him down. The crowd was stunned, nobody expected such a turn of events. The King and his mistress were particularly upset about the failure of their champion.

Jarnac triumphed; he had successfully defended his honour and, in memory of his famous victory, the expression "*coup de Jarnac*" meaning a clever stroke, is still used in French to this day.

Meanwhile La Châtaigneraie, who had prepared a banquet to celebrate his victory, was taken home instead to nurse his wound. Not able to stomach his failure, he removed the bandages and bled to death.

Henri II would certainly have been saddened by his friend's demise, but he endeavoured to forget the whole thing and get on with other affairs.

With Anne de Pisseleu safely out of the way, Diane could now reign unchallenged at court and enjoy being loved so much by the King. He showered her with presents, titles; bestowed on her the Duchy of Étampes (confiscated from Anne de Pisseleu) and the Duchy of Valentinois (previously given to Cesar Borgia, son of pope Alexander VI, by Louis XII in exchange for the annulment of his first marriage). Diane was also offered the crown jewels and a château on the Loire – **Chenonceau,** for 12 years used by his father as a hunting lodge, a very suitable present for a woman who loved hunting as Diane did!

Undoubtedly this château is fit for a lady. And if you look carefully at it, the feminine touch is certainly there. While the grand **Chambord** next door, remarkable for the way it epitomises male prowess and daring with its scale, with its numerous turrets reaching towards the sky and with its ingenious double-helix staircase, it nevertheless lacks comfort and warmth. **Chenonceau** on the other hand with its original five-arched bridge/gallery over the river Cher, albeit built on a much smaller scale, is elegant, pleasant and cosy.

It was Diane de Poitiers who realised the full potential of the mansion. Soon after she received it as a gift from Henri, money not being an issue, she started extensive reconstruction works – had a bridge built over the river, to give her easy access to the hunting grounds beyond, laid out elaborate formal gardens and transformed it into a love nest for herself and her Royal lover.

In her room we can still see their initials on the fireplace and the ceiling – the "H" for Henri and "C" for Catherine are intertwined in such a way as to actually form "D" for Diane inside the "H"…

Diane loved **Chenonceau** and it suited her lifestyle to a T. It is not so surprising that this lady saw her alter ego in Diane, the Huntress, for she had been introduced to hunting by her father from an early age as her legendary namesake would have been and she enjoyed this pastime very much. She favoured hunting with falcons and on her return after a day of hunting in the woods surrounding **Chenonceau**, she would bath naked in the cool waters of the Cher River.

This château was the perfect place of retreat, also a place for pleasure, where balls were organised, tennis was played, art works were admired.

As time went by, Diane, although still in love with the King, was getting more and more involved in politics, using her position to the best advantage of her family and friends. As a result the interests of France were suffering in much the same way as during "the reign" of the previous Duchess of Étampes, Anne de Pisseleu.

Diane's younger daughter was married into the Guise family, so the interest of this family became paramount for the new favourite, never thinking that in giving them so much power, they might one day become a threat to the King himself. But that's exactly what happened in the end; not in Henri's lifetime, but afterwards. However this is all to come. At the time Diane, intoxicated by the influence she had on Henri, was *de facto* ruling the Kingdom of which he was the sovereign in name only.

Catherine de Medici, busy producing children after 10 years of sterility, was conveniently out of the way most of the time and didn't pose any problems. At public events the favourite was unabashedly taking the place of honour without anybody even thinking to challenge her.

Well, almost, if we don't count Anne de Montmorency, the Supreme Commander of the French armies. The owner of that name didn't have anything effeminate about him. Closely involved with the Royal family, Anne got his Christian name from his god mother, who was no other than

Queen Anne of Brittany herself. He was a close friend and ally to François I, but fell out of favour with him thanks to his namesake Anne, the Duchess of Etampes. Later, following the ascent of Henri II, he was back again until the time he crossed swords with the new favourite…and lost.

The Duke had really misjudged the situation in opposing the Guises and managed to seriously annoy Diane further by sending a replacement to the Royal bed while the favourite was stuck at home, recovering from an injury caused by falling from a horse.

So the Duke de Montmorency had to go (let's not feel sorry for him however, the wheel of fortune will turn for him again in the years to come). Thus by alienating the King from a loyal follower, Diane reinforced her authority once again.

The temporary occupant of the Royal bed was actually the governess of the young Mary Stuart, the fiancée of the Dauphin. This brief encounter bore fruit and having given birth to a baby boy, she was duly sent back to her Scottish homeland.

Another war in which Henri II was involved, thanks to Diane and the Guises, did not bring anything good for France, it led to a humiliating peace treaty and the end of the Italian dream; Diane however kept her lands and a County in the Kingdom of Naples.

But all things must pass and finally after 12 years reign, Henri's time was up. He was just 40 years old and what happened was a tragedy. However, as early as 1546, the renowned astrologer Nostradamus had warned Catherine de Medici that the life of the King would be in danger when he reached the age of 40 and he should avoid at all costs to enter into single combat. The following verses, now famous, are an expression of the best known fulfilled prophecy of Nostradamus:

The young lion will overcome the older one,
On the field of combat in a single battle;
He will pierce his eyes through a golden cage,
Two wounds made one, then he dies a cruel death.
(Century 1, Quatrain 35)

In June 1559, Henry II ignored all warnings and during the celebrations for the wedding of his daughter Elisabeth to Philip II of Spain, participated in a jousting tournament against the Count de Montgomery. Both men used shields embossed with lions.

During the final attack, Montgomery's lance shattered, thrusting a large splinter through the King's gilded visor (*golden cage*). Along with minor cuts in the face and throat, there were two mortal wounds. One splinter destroyed the King's eye; the other pierced his temple just behind the eye. Both penetrated his brain. The famous surgeon Ambroise Paré was called but he could not do anything for him. In agony Henry survived ten more days before dying a most horrific death.

CHAPTER 8

The Florentine in Power
Chaumont vs. Chenonceau
(16th century)

Catherine must have been devastated by this calamity but kept a cool head. She took charge of the situation at once. Diane was not allowed at the deathbed of her lover. She must have realised things were going really badly when she received a messenger from the part of Catherine to claim back the crown jewels. However Diane refused to give them up while the King was still living, hoping against all odds for some miracle to happen. But all was in vain. She wasn't allowed to the funeral either.

"The King is dead, long live the King" (*"Le Roi est mort, vive le Roi!"*). After the traditional proclamation, the son of Catherine ascended to the throne under the name of François II. The King was very young. Till the death of his father he had lived with his brothers and sisters in **Blois** and in **Amboise.**

Catherine, heartbroken decided to wear nothing but black from then on, which shocked everybody, because the colour of mourning for the Royals in those times was white. On a portrait by François Clouet, dating from that time, we see her wearing a widow's cap (the so called French hood), a white ruff and a high black collar. She changed her coat of arms to represent a broken lance with the motto: "From there come my tears and my pain" (*«Lacrymae hinc, hinc dolor»*).

In the meantime Catherine received the jewels she'd requested accompanied by a humble letter from her rival. The Queen-mother decided to be magnanimous. She had to tread carefully because the Guises, whose careers Diane had propelled forward, were still very powerful. However the Florentine found a way to humiliate the ex-favourite.

It was all to do with a château; or rather two châteaux. The Queen-mother hadn't forgotten **Chenonceau**, the charming love nest Diane had been given by the late King. She knew she would touch a tender spot if she seized it. To appear generous, she offered her another one in exchange – **Chaumont**.

Chaumont was a château on the Loire that had belonged to the Amboise family. Catherine had acquired it in 1550 not because she was that interested in the château itself, with its austere medieval aspect, not at all to the taste of a refined Renaissance lady, but because the lands that went with it were very lucrative. There were the vineyards, the wine-cellars, the toll-bridge over the Loire, the Royal river itself, all contributed to amass a large revenue.

It does not seem that she stayed there much, but today, the visitor will be shown her room and also the room said to be of her astrologer Ruggieri, because of a cabalistic sign on the fireplace (in fact it is the monogram of Diane de Poitiers) and a portrait believed to represent him.

They say that Ruggieri used to watch the stars from the top of the tower. The 13th century tower at **Blois** is also associated with stargazing – it is claimed that Catherine had her astrological observatory there, because of the sign *Uraniae Sacrum* (the Temple of Urania) which is still visible (Urania was the muse of Astronomy according to Greek mythology; John Milton refers to her as "heavenly muse" in "Paradise Lost").

Did Ruggieri ever stay at **Chaumont**? It's hard to prove one way or the other. It is said that it was at **Chaumont** where Ruggieri (or, according to some sources, Nostradamus himself) predicted the length of the reigns of Catherine's sons, using mirrors which showed their images turning round on themselves; each turn representing a year of reign.

He also predicted the end of the Valois' Dynasty and the advent of Henri IV Bourbon. If those dark predictions were indeed made at that place, it's no wonder that Catherine wanted to exchange it for the joyful **Chenonceau**, despite its connection with the love-affair of Henri II and Diane.

Diane didn't stay long at **Chaumont**. She left it and retired to Anet, to the west of Paris, where she spent the last years of her life. In spite of it all, she was still full of energy and kept her looks. A contemporary of hers who visited her there, wrote that at the age of 70 (she was actually no more than 66), she looked as beautiful and as attractive as if she were still thirty; above all, she had a wonderfully white skin and no need for makeup.

In fact Diane used to go bathing in the river and riding every day to keep fit and to improve her skin colour, every morning she drank some concoction, based on gold, which finally killed her.

Scientists have recently discovered such high concentrations of gold in her hairs that it seems the former favourite had poisoned herself in her determination to remain forever young. She was 66 when she died.

Soon after Catherine had laid her hands on **Chenonceau,** her rival out of the way, she started extensive works on her new property. With her taste for magnificence, not unlike her father–in–law, she wanted to outshine Diane, who had eclipsed her for so long, and to leave her own mark. She also wanted to establish herself as a great patron of the arts, worthy of her predecessors on the Valois and Medici side.

Ironically, **Chenonceau** is the only example of Catherine's endeavours that survives to this day; all the others were demolished in the course of time.

Catherine constructed new outbuildings and had a park laid out, a separate garden as a counterpoint to the one created by Diane. Most importantly, Catherine added a two storey gallery on the bridge over the river Cher, probably inspired by Ponte Vecchio in her native Florence, which makes this château so distinctive. The main gallery, which wasn't finished till 1577, in fact doubled as a ball room, a concept quite unique, not known to exist elsewhere.

To forget the tournaments, so fashionable during her husband's lifetime, that cost him his life, and also to take her away from the tensions, tearing the country apart, the Queen-mother made of **Chenonceau** a palace of pleasure; a palace where festivities were often held, where the so called "flying squadron" (*escadron volant*) operated; consisting of young attractive girls, who seduced but also spied on certain persons, that the Queen-mother didn't trust.

In 1560 Jean Nicot, the French Ambassador to Portugal who was there to negotiate the marriage of the young Princess Marguerite of France with the Portuguese Prince, introduced Catherine de Medici to a new "miracle cure", the tobacco, which although quite popular on the Iberian Peninsula, was still practically unknown to the rest of Europe.

According to some sources she used it to ease the migraines she suffered from, according to others – as a cure for her sickly son, François II. Whatever the truth, the Queen-mother was so impressed by this panacea, that it became known as *"Herbe à la Reine"* (the Queen's herb).

Duke de Guise however proposed to name it *Nicotiana* after Jean Nicot, despite the fact that it was actually another Frenchman, André Thevet who had brought it to France on his return from Brazil, but never got the credit for it. But then he didn't have rich and influential patrons to sing his praises…

Despite her little triumphs, Catherine still had to grapple for position and to take great care at the treacherous Royal court. The young King, being at the age of 15, did not require a Regent; however, due to his inexperience and ill health, he left the maternal uncles of his wife to deal with the important affairs of State.

Those uncles were the powerful Guises (Duke de Guise and his brother Cardinal de Lorraine), the young Queen being of course none other than the (in)famous Mary Stuart, Queen of Scots, daughter of Marie de Guise, sister of the two Guises.

Now, if the Huguenots (French Protestants) hoped that their lot would improve after the demise of Henri II, they must have been sorely disappointed by this development. The Catholic Guises were not very likely to handle them with kid gloves. However on 8th March 1560 the Royal Council, under the influence of Catherine de Medici, decided on an amnesty.

Meanwhile the Huguenots were conspiring to abduct the King, in order to coerce him to embrace their cause and to get rid of the Guises. This plot is now known as the **Amboise** conspiracy. The Guises got wind of it and moved the court from **Blois** to **Amboise,** because they deemed that the château of **Amboise** was better fortified and thus safer.

The conspirators were arrested on arrival and reprisals followed. From the terraces of the **Amboise** château the Royal family watched their enemies being hanged.

After that blood bath, the Royal family, heavily escorted, went to Tours and afterwards to **Chenonceau**, where splendid festivities in honour of the Royal couple took place, to distract them from the gruesome spectacle they had recently witnessed. Music, water displays, fireworks, nothing was spared to impress the guests and make them forget the massacre.

Nevertheless, afterwards, Catherine de Medici, still bent on conciliation, appointed Michel de l'Hospital as Chancellor. A moderate Catholic, he strived towards religious tolerance and towards a reformed Church of France, but despite his efforts all he accomplished was to postpone the Religious Wars for a while. It was almost impossible to convince the fanatics from the two opposing camps to settle their differences.

"You are saying that your religion is the best. I defend mine. What is the most reasonable: that I should follow your opinion, or you – mine?" he pleaded in a discourse at the States General (the equivalent of the Parliament at the time) at Orleans in 1560, "and who will be the judge if not a Council of Saints? Let's do away with the diabolical words, the names of parties, factions, seditions, Lutherans, Huguenots, Papists. Let's not change the name of the Christian."

Amidst the religious tensions in his kingdom, the young King was dying. Not yet 17 years old, he's hardly been 17 months on the throne and no heir produced. Despite the efforts of the best physicians of the time, he expired in December 1560 in Orleans.

Charles, the younger brother of François II, ascended to the throne under the name Charles IX. He was only ten and Catherine made sure that this time she would call the shots. Accordingly she was appointed as Regent and soon afterwards young Mary Stuart was sent packing. The uncles had to withdraw too. From that moment on Catherine de Medici firmly took the reins of power and didn't slacken her pace in the following decades. She could not afford to.

Duke François de Guise and his party were not to be driven out so easily. Nicknamed Scar-face (*Le Balafré*) for a scar he was left with after a battle, he remained a staunch Catholic. They were determined to eradicate the Huguenots and Catherine's more conciliatory line didn't please them. It wasn't difficult to ignite the spark of the first war of Religion, with tensions running so high following the massacre at Wassy that he initiated.

However Duke de Guise lost his life during the conflict, murdered by a fanatical Huguenot at the siege of Orleans. Antoine de Bourbon, Lieutenant-General of the Kingdom of France (the father of the future Henri IV), acting in the name of Charles IX, was also killed by the Protestants at the siege of Rouen. At this point Catherine signed the peace treaty. But it was a very fragile peace that didn't last long.

Trapped between two antagonistic parties, the Queen-mother struggled to maintain the national unity around the throne. The Catholics blamed her for giving too many freedoms to the Huguenots, the Huguenots – for not giving them enough.

She was reproached for changing camps too often. In fact the poor Queen was fighting tooth and nail not only for her own brood, but also for the integrity of the Kingdom and for the future of the Valois dynasty. She didn't trust anybody and played one against the other in an effort to keep the *status-quo*.

Being superstitious didn't help at all. Some of her actions strike us as being, well, inconsistent, but the truth is that she believed in everything that her astrologer, Ruggieri, told her!

The majority of the King is proclaimed in the summer of 1563. The Queen-mother still held her position though. In 1564 she organised a Grand Tour of France for her son, the King. She believed it was important for him to see his Kingdom and for his subjects to see him, in order to maintain the unity of the country.

This tour lasted 2 years and Catherine and Charles IX went around accompanied by 1000 of their followers. The itinerary went through the most troubled towns of France. In places that were mostly Protestant, the King was welcomed with respect, but nothing more. The only hitch was at La Rochelle (and this was to be the last visit of a French King there before 1627) and Orleans, where the cortege was met by riots. Also as **Saumur** was occupied by the Protestant troops of Prince de Condé, the King and the Queen-mother were not able to enter it.

The religious tensions continued on and off. Catherine pursued her grandiose projects both in Paris and in the Loire. There was a widespread discontent amongst the populace for what they saw as being sheer wastefulness. As Ronsard succinctly put it:

> *The Queen must cease building,*
> *Her lime must stop swallowing our wealth…*
> *Painters, masons, engravers, stone-carvers*
> *Drain the treasury with their deceits.*

And the French art historian Jean-Pierre Babelon remarked that "this daughter of the Medici was driven by a passion to build and a desire to leave great achievements behind her when she died."

Catherine de Medici was undoubtedly extravagant and spent beyond her means and yet thanks to her patronage, many artists thrived and produced some of their finest works.

The engravings and drawings of the eminent architect Jacques Androuet du Cerceau, who worked under her and her husband's patronage, testify to the great progress of French Renaissance architecture at the time.

Henri II and Catherine de Medici had commissioned him to produce engravings of the most sumptuous buildings in their kingdom, a very ambitious project, and he surpassed himself, creating a masterpiece – an album in colour, dedicated to Catherine de Medici -"The most excellent buildings of France", consisting of 116 engravings carefully executed on vellum, which include amongst others, the châteaux of **Blois**, **Chambord** and **Chenonceau.**

This was a work of art far ahead of its time, which interestingly ended up in the British museum. In a period, when neither photography nor aeronautics existed and at least two centuries were to elapse before the Montgolfier brothers came up with the idea of the hot air balloon, Androuet du Cerceau produced engravings depicting bird's eye views of the great Renaissance châteaux. One could see the towers of **Chambord** in detail, the fortifications of

Amboise before they were dismantled, the château of **Blois** and its gardens.

He drew the plan of the ground floor of the residential part of **Chenonceau** sometime before 1579. There exists also a plan of the proposed future extensions of the château and grounds, done for Catherine de Medici. From this plan we can see that it was to be even more grandiose and on a yet bigger scale, but for whatever reason (presumably lack of sufficient funds), it was never realised.

However some works did continue and the château gradually took on the aspect that we know today.

An alley, bordered with magnificent plane trees leads to the château. One can imagine Charles IX entering amidst sirens, nymphs, satyrs. After passing between two sphinxes, the visitor has to cross the draw bridge to find themselves at the terrace, surrounded by the moat. To the left is Diane's Italian garden, to the right – Catherine's, encircled by the big trees of the park. In the middle of the terrace towers the keep, the only reminder of the ancient medieval fortress.

Today there is a room particularly associated with Catherine de Medici and another one (the room of the five Queens) – with her daughters: Elisabeth (Queen of Spain), Marguerite (Queen of Navarre and France) and her daughters-in-law, who succeeded each other as Queens of France: Mary Stuart, Elisabeth of Austria and Louise of Lorraine.

Catherine enjoyed beautifying her château and entertaining her visitors there.

But what Charles IX mostly enjoyed, was hunting and …working in his smithy. Despite his delicate constitution the King used to hunt for as long as 10 hours at a time, repeatedly spitting blood and tiring up to 5 horses in the process.

But as time went by, Charles started to take more and more interest in the politics of his Kingdom. His brother, Henri d'Anjou, acting as his Lieutenant-General won a couple of important battles against the Protestants (Jarnac and Moncontour) and was acclaimed as a hero. Perhaps there was jealousy on account of these victories. Whatever the reason, Charles started to act on his own without consulting the Queen-mother.

The King initiated diplomatic steps to improve relations with England and the Holy Roman Empire. He married Elisabeth of Austria, the daughter of the Holy Roman Emperor, Maximilien II and Mary of Spain, the Spanish Infanta. The only fruit of this union was a girl and sadly the poor child died young. However Charles' mistress, Marie Touchet, gave him a son, named after him, Charles de Valois, later known as the Duke of Angouleme.

The King also strived towards a more permanent reconciliation with the Huguenots and established amicable relations with Admiral Coligny, one of their leaders. And of course there was also the matter of the marriage of his sister, Margot, to the Prince of Navarre, Henri. This Prince was the grandson of the sister of François I, who also happened to be called Marguerite, which makes Henri and Margot cousins.

Their wedding was preceded by lengthy and tortuous negotiations between their respective mothers: the formidable Jeanne d'Albret, Queen of Navarre and her worthy counterpart Catherine de Medici. One of their meetings to discuss the marriage was held at **Chenonceau**.

It was finally agreed that Marguerite was to keep her Catholic faith despite the official religion of Navarre being Protestantism (a generous dowry was to compensate for that concession). This purely political alliance preceded by only a few days the St. Bartholomew's massacre.

The notorious Margot was truly a Renaissance child – gorgeous, smart, brilliantly educated and…born ahead of her time. She is immortalised by Dumas in "The Queen Margot" (La Reine Margot").

Marguerite's story is really tragic. She had fallen in love with the young Duke de Guise, a Prince of Royal blood (he claimed Carolingian descent) and he would have married her if it wasn't for her mother, Catherine de Medici, and Charles IX, who was on the throne at the time, both violently opposed to such a union. Had she married the Duke, the history of France might have been very different.

As it was, Margot had to grit her teeth and go through with a marriage she didn't want and be united with a husband she was indifferent to. But in those times arranged marriages were the norm, especially in Royal households.

Margot became the Queen of Navarre, but life wasn't very easy for her. As a Catholic, she would have felt a bit out of place at the Protestant court of Navarre, although she was allowed to practise her faith. Her husband didn't care a lot for her but unashamedly used her every time he needed her help. He was a lady's man *par excellence* and would even sleep with her ladies in waiting if he felt like it.

Margot also had her flings to be sure, but of course in those times, a woman had to be much more careful when having an affair. It seems that at some point she must have been well passed caring.

After a quarrel with her husband she eloped with an officer of her guard. Margot got caught between the Devil and the deep blue sea, for her brother Henri, who didn't get on with her (despite some nasty rumours that she had slept with him and indeed all her brothers), was trying to capture her and have her sent back to her husband; exhausted and ill, she appealed to her mother, who lured her to one of her châteaux and then sent her to another one, where she was to remain a virtual prisoner till the end of her brother's reign. But that is another story.

Historians have never agreed on the real purpose of that marriage. Some maintain that it was mainly to attract the Huguenots to the capital for the festivities in order to finish them off once and for all. Surely it couldn't be as simple as that. Catherine de Medici was trying a line of appeasement with the Huguenots.

Henri Bourbon, their leader, was after all the King of Navarre, a small autonomous Kingdom which never the less remained under French influence (not unlike Monaco today), but he was also next in line to the French throne, after the Valois brothers. It made sense for him to marry into the family and keep de Guise out of the picture.

The infamous St. Bartholomew night that followed the wedding, was a tragic but inevitable development of the escalating conflict between the two main religions in the Kingdom. It was preceded by a failed attempt to murder Admiral Gaspard de Coligny, one of the Protestant leaders for whom King Charles had lately shown high regard. The King went to see him on his sick bed and promised him justice.

Charles IX must have been persuaded in the meantime that a Protestant uprising was imminent, in order for him to change so drastically his whole attitude and to sanction not just the execution of the wounded man, but the whole St. Bartholomew operation. He must have given the orders for the execution of the most prominent Huguenot leaders, perhaps pressured by his mother and/or by the Guises and scared by the Huguenot army led by Coligny's brother-in-law, camping just outside the city walls?

Catherine de Medici was implicated of course, but it's impossible to say how much she was involved in the blood bath that eradicated so many Huguenots, for the scale of it would not have been to her liking at all. Certainly the Guises were the executors of this massacre, but were they also the organisers? In a pro-Catholic Paris their actions would have been taken as an example to follow, causing a snowball effect.

In front of the Paris Parliament, Charles IX declared that he had done it in order to prevent a Huguenot plot against the Royal family. His tragic end soon afterwards was seen by some at the time as a just retribution for this appalling deed. Justly or unjustly, today he is mostly remembered as the weak King who sanctioned the massacre of Saint Bartholomew night.

CHAPTER 9

The War of the Three Henries (16th century)

Blois – the château we see today is an impressive presentation of architecture going back four centuries. At the time of Catherine de Medici and her brood it had quite a different aspect. The Gaston d'Orleans wing was not built yet; the François I wing, built by the father-in-law of Catherine, was facing not the street, but extensive gardens, laid out by Louis XII and extended by François I. This was the façade of the loggias, so called because of the numerous loggias and balconies on that side. It was inspired by a façade, built by Bramante in the Vatican.

Viewed from the courtyard, one can fully appreciate how remarkable this wing is, due to the great spiral staircase with its loggia like openings at each turn that contrast with the massive structure of the building. The *mise en scène* was such as to allow one "to see and to be seen", that is from the courtyard the courtesans could see the King going up or down the stairs, but also from the open bays they could watch spectacles, performed down in the courtyard.

This staircase was then at the centre of the façade, but at a later time the left part of the wing was demolished to allow for works on the Gaston d'Orleans wing. But even if it had been left the way it was, there was little symmetry to the composition; in those times the openings for the windows were placed wherever deemed appropriate, depending on the functions and exigencies of the particular room they belonged to.

The decoration of the façade and the staircase was also inspired by Italian models and is typical of the early French Renaissance. Numerous Royal emblems adorn the façade – from the crowned salamanders of François to the monograms "F" and "C" for the names of the King and the Queen respectively (François and Claude).

Henri, the younger brother of Charles IX, was in Poland when he heard the news of his demise. He had been elected as King of Poland, but he didn't waste any time returning (which leaves us in no doubt as to which throne he preferred). Escorted by just a few trusted friends, he secretly left his palace in Krakow before his Royal subjects were wise to the fact. He didn't feel safe until he crossed the Austrian border. Henri, now Henri III, didn't return straight to Paris though; reassured, he passed through Italy, without undue haste, to see his mother's homeland.

Invited to lavish banquets, which he thoroughly enjoyed, he was impressed by the Italian style as much as his predecessors had been. He even re-introduced the fork to France, an implement hardly known there previously, though his mother, Catherine, had introduced it already at the time she arrived in her adoptive country.

It should not be such a surprise that the young King should feel so excited about a piece of cutlery; if we look at what the fashion was like in those times, especially the wearing of the so called *collerettes*, known in England as a ruff, which were enormous starched, frilled or pleated circular collars of lace, muslin, or other fine fabric, worn by men and women, we'll understand what a challenging task it would have been to insert food in one's mouth in an elegant way without soiling one's collar using just a spoon or knife.

We have to say that Henri III was a bit of a dandy; of course this purely English term had yet to be coined, which didn't happen for another couple of centuries...

Finally the King crossed back into France and, impatient to see Princess de Clèves, the woman he was in love with, he intended to ride directly to Paris, but affairs of State prevented him. Catherine de Medici met him in Lyon. She discouraged her son from acting impulsively. So he remained there for awhile, because of the unrest in the south of France.

Despite this, Henri was already thinking of how to obtain a divorce for the Princess de Clèves, who was married to Prince de Condé, so he could then marry her himself. Alas, "the best laid schemes o' mice an' men gang aft agley" as the poet says.

The Princess died in childbirth and he received the news when he arrived in Avignon. He was devastated (his mother didn't dare to give him the letter personally but left it amongst the papers he was due to look at that morning). He refused to eat for ten days and went into mourning which shocked the court.

However after his consecration at Reims in February 1575, Henri III married Louise de Vaudémont, a Princess from the Lorraine, who he had met on his way to Poland and for whom he had developed a high regard. Unlike other Royal marriages, this one was not made for political reasons; the King was genuinely very fond of his wife and she loved him too. Sadly their union didn't result in any offspring. It didn't stop Henri chasing after other skirts either.

Apparently, despite various rumours hinting at his homosexuality, throughout his life he was obsessed with women and had quite a few flings, but following his marriage, he endeavoured to conduct his affairs more discretely.

As for the alleged homosexuality, those rumours were mostly started by his enemies. Henri was a refined, intelligent man who despite having an excellent reputation as a swordsman and despite his war victories was in fact not at all bloodthirsty, unlike his late brother Charles IX. He felt happier to preside over a council rather than lead a military campaign or hunting expedition.

At a time when warriors were seen as role models, an elegant, educated monarch with refined taste, organising balls and surrounding himself with fashionable men (the so called *mignons*), might be seen by the bourgeoisie as a bit of a pouf; or at least that's how his enemies portrayed him in pamphlets, but there is no other evidence to support this.

The Protestants however disapproved of such a frivolous lifestyle and were the first to associate this trend with homosexuality.

The Catholic League on the other hand was behind the Duke de Guise, Henri's eternal rival, nicknamed like his father Scar-face (*Le Balafré*) for the scar left from a wound attained during a battle. They saw the King as being too weak, too accommodating towards the Protestants, in short – too effeminate. Latter day artists and writers also used this image while portraying Henri III. And so that's how he is remembered, which is a pity.

The *mignons* he surrounded himself with originated mainly from the gentry and not from the ranks of the high aristocracy. They *were* indeed faithful to the King, which no doubt upset the upper crust. Following the King's example the *mignons* spent time on their appearance, wore makeup, earrings, lace…that's to say they determined the fashion at court.

This didn't affect their male prowess. They were kept busy. A lot was happening at the French court; as always there was scandal, intrigue.

This is the place to relate the exploits of Louis de Bussy d'Amboise, another well-known figure from the great Amboise family. This dashing cavalier, who distinguished himself in the religious wars under the Royal banner, who took part in the St. Bartholomew's massacre and who followed the future King Henri III to Poland, had become his favourite.

"He was a man of invincible courage, ease, proud and audacious, as valiant as his sword," Pierre L'Estoile, the chronicler, says about him in his diary.

He might have been fearless, but he was also very well educated, fluent in Greek and Latin, which attracted the attention of the beautiful Margot, the King's sister and wife of the King of Navarre. As we mentioned earlier, this brilliant young woman had received an excellent education (she was also fluent in Greek and Latin) and enjoyed the company of cultured men, who would woo her in Latin perhaps? There was a liaison between the two young people for some time which like every such thing at court, did not remain secret for long.

Bussy's rise to fame was so swift and easy, as to make him even more arrogant. This in turn contributed to his downfall. One of the most popular *mignons* at court, at one point he left the King, his benefactor, to offer his services to *Monsieur*, the Duke d'Alençon, the youngest brother of Henri III. Was it on account of Margot? After all her youngest brother was said to be her favourite.

Thus Bussy got involved in the tensions at court that existed between the King and his brother. Provoking the other *mignons* is what he enjoyed, even if he had to fight duels with them afterwards. Once, after being ordered to make up with one of them, "he entered the Louvre for that reconciliation, accompanied by more than two hundred gentlemen," wrote Brantôme, the writer, in his memoirs, "and it was declared in the presence of the King: "that's a bit excessive for a Bussy."

Bussy was the main participant in a macabre melodrama (or shall we say a tragedy in the classical Greek style?) that took place in the château of Montsoreau. This time it involved the wife of the Lord of Montsoreau, Françoise de Maridor. Her husband, Charles de Chambres, Count of Montsoreau, spent a lot of time at court in Paris, while she stayed either in their château at **Saumur**, either in the château de **Montsoreau** which is also situated on the banks of the Loire.

At that time (1576) this handsome Don Juan, Bussy, was appointed a governor of Anjou and Commander of the château of **Angers**, which the Duke d'Alençon had just received as part of his fiefdom. Bussy led a life of pleasure and debauchery there.

The beautiful Lady of Montsoreau attracted him and, the château of **Montsoreau** being at an easy distance from Angers, he started to visit her; he then had the imprudence to boast about his conquest in writing. The King, Henri III, who was less than impressed with his former favourite, got hold of that letter and showed it to the deceived and cheated husband, who as we can imagine was not impressed in the slightest. The hint was given to the deceived husband that if he were to successfully defend his honour and if the offender were to be killed, there would be no proceedings against him...

The Count of Montsoreau dashed back home and threatened his wife, who had to admit to her infidelity.

He then forced her to arrange a rendezvous with her lover. Bussy d'Amboise duly arrived, but instead of his belle, he found an angry husband backed up by his armed men. His luck had finally run out. Bussy fought valiantly; it is said that he didn't give up, even when his sword broke, but was overwhelmed by the sheer number of his assailants.

However unbelievable it may sound, the Count and his wife made up after this sombre episode and lived happily ever after and had many children.

Bussy was immortalised by the English playwright George Chapman in the Tragedy of Bussy d'Ambois (1607) and later in The Lady of Montsoreau (*La Dame de Montsoreau*) by Alexander Dumas.

King Henri III spent less time in the Loire valley than his predecessors had done. Paris had become again the centre of the Kingdom, though the Loire still remained a favourite place of retreat for him and his court.

Henri III didn't produce any offspring. *Monsieur* (Prince François Duke of Alençon/ Duke of Anjou), was to be his heir. The youngest of the Valois dynasty, he was the only one without a crown despite all his efforts to install himself on a throne, any throne, even the Dutch throne, to which he was invited by William of Orange (the Taciturn); a Treaty to that effect was in fact signed in **Plessis-lés-Tours** in 1580.

At about the same time he was courting Queen Elizabeth I of England, twice his age, and even went on a visit across the Channel but not withstanding his popularity with the Virgin Queen (she used to call him tenderly "my frog") nothing came of it. Ultimately all this scheming was in vain and his untimely death at the age of 29 put again the question of the French succession back on the agenda in 1584.

The next in line was the King of Navarre, Henri Bourbon, a Protestant, well at least at that moment, for Henri Bourbon was not exactly seen as a man with strong religious convictions. He had already changed his religion a couple of times to suit changing circumstances. His mother had imposed Protestantism as the State religion of her little Kingdom of Navarre, much to the disapproval of his father, Antoine de Bourbon, who remained a Catholic till the end.

On his return to Navarre, after years spent in Paris, Henri Bourbon preserved Protestantism as the State religion the way his mother wanted it, and kept his subjects happy.

But if the Protestants were pleased at the prospect of having a Protestant King of France, the Catholics would not have any of it.

The Catholic League was not prepared to accept a heretic for a King, come what may, and they were going to fight over it. It's clear that by that time the Duke de Guise had become the bane of the King's life. This powerful Prince was gradually taking over the country while the poor monarch was gradually losing his influence.

Henri III had to decide which side to take, which wasn't an easy task. Caught between the Devil and the deep blue sea, he was trying to keep the equilibrium, the way his mother had done for years, but that wasn't possible anymore. Duke de Guise, more and more arrogant as time went by, cajoled him into an uneasy alliance; an alliance where the Duke was calling the shots and the King was little by little losing ground.

So this period was dominated by the rivalry between the three Henries and is known as the War of the three Henries.

Let's not forget that Henri Bourbon was married to Princess Marguerite, otherwise known as Margot, the sister of Henri III. At that time she was in exile, enforced on her by her brother in order to keep her out of trouble. It wasn't just her amorous affairs that scandalised the court, but also her political dabbling that was embarrassing to the King.

As we know already, her relations with each of the three parties concerned here were, let's say, somewhat complicated – a brother, a husband and an old flame/rejected candidate. The thought of this woman, plotting and scheming in the background, must have made all of them feel, at least a tiny bit, uncomfortable.

But there was a crown at stake. Worn by one, coveted by the other two, each of them ambitious, each of them eligible to wear it, neither prepared to give up, how long was it going to take before a dramatic finale?

It was the King who lost his nerve in the end. Duke de Guise was wearing him down. The Duke had gained huge popularity in Paris where the people were predominantly Catholic. Henri de Guise was proclaimed the King of Paris by the populace. Forced to flee from the capital, Henri III decided it was time to cut the Gordian knot once and for all.

But what was to be done in order to save the throne of France? What if he somehow managed to throw de Guise into prison, though even that was unlikely to save him, it would be in his own words "like putting a wild boar in nets, stronger than the strings that held him." He had to think of a more drastic plan of action.

The year was 1588. In October the King, Henri III convened the States General (which in those times was the equivalent of Parliament) in the château of **Blois,** where he was living at the time. Once again a Valois King back in the Loire valley where his predecessors had found refuge in similar circumstances.

The Catholic League had a majority and Duke de Guise was preparing a new stratagem against the King. On the 17 December, Cardinal de Guise, his brother, who was representing the clergy at the States General, hopeful that they would be able to dispose of Henri III, had the audacity even to drink a toast in honour of the Duke with the words: "I drink for the health of the King of France!"

Duke de Guise knew he was treading on dangerous ground, yet he didn't care. Some well-wisher actually warned him in a note that the Duke found hidden under his napkin at the dinner table. It read: "Beware of the danger; they are about to get you." He wrote underneath: "They won't dare."

Just before Christmas, on the 23 December, early in the morning, at the time when the Council was about to start its proceedings, the King summoned the Duke to his old office. The Duke promptly went.

To get to that office he had to pass through the bedroom of the King. Eight gentlemen from the so called "Forty five", the King's bodyguard, were concealed in that room. The Duke reached the door of the office and knocked but didn't get an answer. Did he realise that there was something wrong?

In fact, the King was waiting in his new office. But on his way back through the King's room, Duke de Guise was attacked by the King's bodyguard who slaughtered him there and then. He tried to defend himself but of course he didn't stand a chance and fell at the foot of the King's bed.

A note was found on the body of the Duke, in his own handwriting, saying: "To maintain the war in France, 700 000 pounds/livres are needed every month"

To this day the chateau of **Blois** preserves the memory of this macabre event. There is a room there, called Salle de Guise, formerly the room for the Kings' guards, where various paintings are displayed, all depicting the protagonists in this drama. The assassination itself was never painted, but instead, there is the famous picture by Charles Durupt, where the King is portrayed standing with his foot, placed on the Duke's body.

The legend says that when Henri III saw the dead body of his enemy, he exclaimed: "He looks even taller now he is dead, than when he was alive!"

The King then went to his mother, Catherine de Medici and told her cheerfully: "I no longer have a companion, the King of Paris is dead!" "God grant," replied Catherine, "that you have not become the King of nothing at all! Well cut, but it has to be stitched back up now."

The King then went to mass in the St.Calais Chapel.

The body of the Duke was burnt in the château and the ashes were thrown in the Loire…

The King had to deal of course, with the rest of the family; Louis (Cardinal de Guise) and young Charles, respectively the brother and the son of the late Duke, were arrested the next day. The Cardinal was executed on the following day.

Meanwhile Catherine de Medici, who was not informed beforehand of her son's intentions, had to accept the *"fait accompli"*. She felt uneasy, especially because she had put in a lot of effort to reconcile him with Duke de Guise and had thought that she had succeeded.

At the time she was busy with the preparation for the wedding of her favourite granddaughter, Christine de

Lorraine, with another of her Medici relatives – the grand-Duke of Tuscany and a murder wasn't exactly what she had been contemplating.

Worn out by worries, Catherine de Medici succumbed to a cold and passed away soon after, on the 5th January 1589. Her astrologer, Ruggieri, had foretold years earlier that she was going to die near Saint Germain. The poor Queen abandoned the works she had instigated at the palace of Tuileries in the parish of St. Germain l'Auxerrois in Paris and moved quickly to what was to become l'Hotel de la Reine.

She must have felt safe in **Blois** but she couldn't escape her fate and on her death bed when she asked the name of her confessor, from whom she had just received the Last Sacraments, he replied: Julien de Saint Germain.

In spite of her influence on the political life of France over the decades, her death went almost unnoticed. "No sooner had she died, she was shown no more consideration than a goat," wrote the chronicler L'Estoile. The Queen-mother was buried at Blois because Paris was still held by the League.

Apart from **Chenonceau**, nothing is left today of the grandiose works of Catherine de Medici. **Chenonceau** was bequeathed to her daughter-in-law, Louise de Lorraine.

Henri III followed his mother to the grave a few months later. As they say: "Live by the sword, die by the sword".

The King had united forces with the King of Navarre to fight the Catholic League whose strength hadn't diminished after the demise of the Duke de Guise; his younger brother, Duke de Mayenne, who had been at his estates in Burgundy at the time of the reprisals, headed for Paris soon afterwards, where he replaced his late brother; he became the new leader of the League and the whole of France was in uproar.

Preparing to lay a siege on Paris, occupied by the Catholic League, Henri III was attacked by a Dominican monk, who under the pretext of bringing him some important news, stabbed him with a knife, while he was reading the letter brought by the monk. The King drew the knife out himself, reportedly with the words: "Bad monk, you've killed me!" He died the next day and with him died the Valois Dynasty.

At the time of his death, Pierre de l'Estoile, a chronicler, said of him that "he would have been a good Prince, had he known a better century". Maybe in a different century he would not have met with such a violent death, but it was precipitated by his own foolishness in relation to the Duke de Guise. Before his death he appointed Henri of Navarre as his successor.

Louise de Lorraine, the widow of Henri III retired to **Chenonceau**. Inconsolable, she spent the rest of her life there (she outlived her husband by 11 years), wearing white clothes as a sign of mourning (for which the local peasants nicknamed her the White Queen – *La Reine Blanche*). Her rooms were all covered in black velvet with curtains made of black damask; crowns, thorns and Franciscan girdles were painted in white on black ceilings.

After her death the château passed to César de Vendôme, the bastard son of the King of Navarre, who had married her niece, the rich heiress Françoise de Lorraine.

It took Henri of Navarre another five years or so to take Paris. The capital was still in the hands of the Leaguers at the time of his consecration in 1594, but the popular mood was changing and the Parisians were becoming more and more favourable to the new King.

In March, Henri IV sent one of his confidants to the governor of Paris, the Count de Brissac, to negotiate terms for surrendering the city. To coerce him towards his cause, the Count was offered a goodly amount of money and a field marshal's baton.

The offer was tempting, so on the 22 March, a few companies of Royal soldiers quietly infiltrated the city and occupied strategic points. When the King presented himself at *Porte Neuve* (the present day *Pont du Carrousel*) he was welcomed by the Count de Brissac and was handed the keys to the city. Henri IV honoured the Count with the title Marshal of France as promised and took possession of his capital.

Count de Brissac later obtained a ducal crown. The money he received, he invested in his château **Brissac** in the Loire valley. He started to build a sumptuous residence there worthy of his status. However the money wasn't sufficient to finish it off. The result is an interesting mixture of styles that never the less works beautifully; as his descendant, the present Duke and owner aptly put it: "A new château not completed in an old castle only half destroyed."

But this was yet to happen during this Bourbon era. The Dynasty Henri of Navarre founded is known as the Bourbon Dynasty and Henri IV, himself was also known as *le Vert Galant*, roughly translated in English as The Old Spark (this nickname was an allusion to his many love affairs).

Henri IV divorced his wife Marguerite of France, sister of Henri III, but remained on friendly terms with her till the end. Ironically, following the divorce, he then married a relative of hers from the Medici family – Marie de Medici, and in the space of 10 years produced 6 children. We are not counting here the illegitimate children he had from other women.

This is the end of our travels in the Loire valley of the Valois. The Bourbons did not appreciate it and centred their life on Paris and its environs. But like the Sleeping Beauty it has been awaken from its sleep and tempts us now to go and explore its many secrets. Who knows, maybe we'll meet there again.

APPENDIX

Loire. The River. The Vineyards.
The Setting for the Renaissance Châteaux.

The all important first impression was not at all what I would call favourable and yet I will never forget this moment. It happened a long time ago in Nantes, just before the great river reaches the ocean at St. Nazaire. I can still see in my mind's eye the murky brown waters lazily flowing between dishevelled bushy river banks.

Then there is another image, in Nantes again, some 17 years or so later; at the very instant when the sun finally makes an appearance on a particularly foggy autumnal morning, I have this eerie feeling, while I walk across the bridge over the muddy waterway and everything around seeming unreal, as under a spell.

In the meantime, the Loire had already told me some of her stories. But there are plenty more for me to discover, each one more fascinating than the previous one.

Even the name Loire sounds somewhat romantic, perhaps because it makes you think of Lorelei, the siren from the German legend, who lured sailors with her songs on the river Rhine to their doom.

Alas there is no romantic story here. In fact the name Loire is of a Celtic/Gaulish origin and was transliterated as *Liger* in Latin. *Liger* itself comes from *"liga"*, a Gaulish term for sediment, alluvium, deposit.

When the French refer to the climate of the Loire, *climat ligérien*, they imply that it is milder in winter with no extreme temperatures. The Loire is perceived as the dividing line between the northern and southern weather systems in France.

There is something special about the way the light affects the landscape emphasizing the blue skies over the usually calm waters of the Loire and its tributaries, the green valleys and the sunny slopes with fertile vineyards.

Indeed the vineyards here always stretch along the waterways: along the Loire, Cher, Indre, Allier, Vienne, Layon, Aubance, Sèvre Nantaise, Maine. The reason for this is to be protected from the cold in spring and autumn and to find coolness in summer. Besides the sunlight reflects on the water surface, releasing more warmth.

Those vineyards produce excellent wines: dry aromatic Sancerre wines, fruity varieties from around Orleans and Blois, sweet and heady wines from Anjou and great vintages from Touraine.

The vine was of course introduced to France by the Romans in antiquity.

There was a real expansion during the time of Henry II Plantagenet, Count of Anjou, when he became King of England in 1154. He had his wines from Anjou served at his court in England, a tradition followed by his successors, John Lackland and Henry III.

Throughout the centuries the Capets, the Plantagenets, the Valois, in short all the crowned heads of England and France, contributed to build the reputation of the wines of the Loire.

Good King René of Anjou wrote that of all the wines in his wine-cellar; coming from his vineyards in Anjou, Lorraine and Provence, the best ones were from Anjou.

But the golden age of winemaking was, as you might have guessed, the Renaissance. One of the reasons was that when the court of François I was moving from one château to another, in order to fully enjoy and appreciate the place, each had to have its own vineyard and its own style of wine. Therefore the wines from the Loire were at the centre of wine-producing in France.

In his writings François Rabelais attests that the wines of Chinon were favoured at the court of the Valois.

In the Loire valley we are really in the world of Pantagruel and Gargantua, where the wines are worthy of Rabelais himself – popular yet sophisticated at the same time.

Another reason for their success was the lack of secure roads in those times. The Loire offered an ideal way to transport them. Angers and Nantes were the ports where spices were imported and wines were exported. Paris was then, as it is today, the ideal market for the wines of the Loire.

The Loire is the longest river in France, its length is about 1000 km or so and for millennia it was a major thoroughfare of the country, until the coming of the railway in the 19th century.

Along the 1000 kilometres from the Ardeche to the Atlantic, the grand river has decided to indulge us with six great winegrowing areas, alternating the colours of the soils and the wines.

A viticulturist with a poetic streak says that from the source to the estuary of the Loire the dry white wines and the reds correspond to the structure of a sonnet written by someone from the Pleïade. On the two extremities are the dry whites – the Sancerre in the east and the Muscadet in the west. Then from side to side the three expressions of the Chenin vine – the Vouvray in the east, the Savenniers and Coteaux du Layon in the west.

Of course the Loire valley is somewhat to the north so as not to be suitable for vineyards producing red wines, which need more sunshine and warmth. That's why the white wines dominate here.

A French explorer, called Bernard Ollivier at the age of seventy decided to follow the river by turns walking or by canoe, all the way from its source to its estuary at St. Nazaire (just outside Nantes) with wine-tasting of course.

He described his adventures on the river in a book, published recently in French *"Aventures en Loire"*.

Apparently the Loire has not just one, but three sources – each of them with a claim to be "the real one": the" veritable", the "geographic" and the "authentic" and after seeing all three of them, Ollivier gave up on the idea of trying to settle the question of which one was The Source.

As for me, after sifting through loads of information, I have given up on the idea of finding out the exact number of castles in the Loire valley. The number 800 is the best I can come up with and that's no more than a guess.

But how to count them? Let's make it clear that what is meant by the term "The Châteaux of the Loire" are those castles that are situated in the valley of the river from Sancerre to Nantes, no matter whether they are by the Loire itself or by one of its tributaries; that includes even those that are further afield like Châteaudun or Valençay.

Why the château of Nantes is not included in the list is anybody's guess…I have included it in my list, not just because it is situated on the Loire itself, but also because it is the Château of Anne de Bretagne, twice a Queen of France and a major figure in our story.

It is such an impressive fortification and it's not surprising that when Henri IV visited Nantes in 1598 to sign the edict of Nantes, thus marking the end of nearly 30 years of religious wars between Catholics and Huguenots, at the view of it he exclaimed: "God's teeth! No small potatoes our cousins of Brittany"

The Châteaux of the Loire – Royal Palaces and Residences of some of the Protagonists of this Story

Chinon. Perched on a spur overlooking the Vienne River, situated superbly at the crossroads of the provinces of Anjou, Poitou and Touraine, this extensive Royal fortress dominates the town.
Built to withstand sieges, the château grew with the successive works of the Dukes of Blois, the Dukes of Anjou/ the Plantagenets (the greater part of the castle was built by Henry Plantagenet) and eventually the Kings of France.

It witnessed the death of Henry II Plantagenet, the King of England in 1189. It was taken in 1205 after a long siege by Philippe-Auguste. It imprisoned in its cells the Knights Templar, including their Grand Master Jacques de Molay; he was held in the *Tour de Coudray* (interestingly Joan of Arc would be lodged in the same place).

Abandoned by the court, the château was left in disrepair. Cardinal Richelieu bought it and his family kept it until the French Revolution. Now, after 4 years of restoration, it attracts more and more tourists to the town.

Amboise. The ridge on which the chateau stands has been fortified from the Gallo-Roman period. A bridge has existed there since those times which increased the importance of the town. Having been compromised by his involvement in a plot against Georges de La Trémoille, the Chamberlain of Charles VII, Louis d'Amboise, the owner of the domain, was imprisoned and the château confiscated. (see **Montsoreau**).

It is the birth place of Charles VIII and was a principal Royal residence both during his reign (he died there in 1498) and during the early years of the reign of François I; the home of Francois I from his early childhood (he lived there with his mother and his sister Marguerite de Valois).

This château was the first architectural expression of the Renaissance in the Loire Valley; sadly, it has been partly demolished at a later period. Charles VIII did a lot of work on it, extended it and brought an Italian designer to lay the garden parterre and bring water up from the Loire to it. Louis XII built a gallery round it; which can be seen in the famous 1576 engraving by Jacques Androuet Cerceau.

Later François I and his son Henri II would pursue works on the château, following the Italian trends of the time. **Clos-Lucé** (near **Amboise**), a red brick manor house was acquired by Charles VIII in 1490. He had a chapel added for his wife, Anne of Brittany. Later, François I lived at the manor house with his mother and sister. The château is best known as the last home of Leonardo da Vinci who was installed there by the King himself; the great artist died in 1519 and was buried in the Chapel St. Hubert in the château Amboise.

Blois belonged to the Counts of Blois (the neighbours and rivals of the Counts of Anjou) from the 10th till the 14th century. The county was acquired by the brother of Charles VI, Louis, the Duke of Orleans at the end of the 14th century; thereafter the court of Orleans was held in **Blois**. After the assassination of the Duke of Orleans by his cousin the Duke of Burgundy, Louis' inconsolable widow Valentina Visconti retired to **Blois**. According to some guide books she had her motto carved on the walls: "*Plus ne m'est rien, rien n'est me plus*" ("Nothing matters to me anymore"); but this is a misconception. In those times ladies expressed their sentiments in a much more symbolic fashion, rather than adopting the crude ways of mere prisoners. In fact she had the so called *Larmier d'or,* (golden droplets), mixed with peacock feathers (called "regrets") painted on the walls of her apartments. Initially the symbol of the tears that the Virgin Mary shed at the crucifixion of Christ, the *larmier d'or* was later used to express more personal bereavement.

Blois became the principal Royal residence with the ascent of Louis XII (the grandson of Valentina Visconti) to the throne and retained its importance throughout the reigns of the *Valois* Kings until the murder of the Duke de Guise in 1588.

Angers. A castle was built there by the formidable Foulque Nerra, Count of Anjou, an ancestor of Henry Plantagenet; Saint Louis rebuilt it between 1228 and 1238. In the 14th and 15th centuries it was the seat of the Dukes of Anjou. Louis II Duke of Anjou, his wife Yolande d'Aragon and their son and heir, remembered fondly as Good King René (he was the King of Naples, Jerusalem and Sicily) and his young wife known as good Queen Jeanne held court there. King Charles VII of France, their in-law, frequently stayed at the castle as well.

Situated on a rocky promontory, this formidable citadel is in a highly strategic position, dominating the town and the River Maine below. When you enter it you appreciate how vast the place is – laid out over more than 20000 sq. m. the fortress is bounded by a curtain wall with 17 mighty towers, built of alternate layers of dark schist and white limestone. *Le Logis Royal* (the Royal residence) is all that remains of the residential wings, built by Louis II, Duke of Anjou, in the 14th century.

His son René added a gallery to it in 1450. Next to it is a gothic-angevin style chapel, built around 1410 by Yolande d'Aragon, René's mother. *Le logis de Governeur* (The Governor's residence, the staircase turret of which dates from the 15th century) is situated opposite, along the castle wall.

René was the last of the Dukes. His nephew, King Louis XI, annexed the château to the crown, forcing him to retire to his lands in Provence. Louis XI built the moats in 1485. Later on, in 1562, Catherine de Medici had the fortress restored, but her son Henri III had the height of the towers reduced and the towers and walls striped of their battlements; terraces were created to give the defenders a clear field of fire. The stone was then used to pave the streets of Angers.

Saumur Several fortresses succeeded each other on this steep headland. The present château was built in the 14th century by Louis I, Duke of Anjou and finished by Louis II. The interior was redone in the 15th century by Good King René, Duke of Anjou, who also decorated it in the late gothic style. It has been depicted like that as the September miniature in the Very Rich Hours of Duke de Berry, the illuminated manuscript we've mentioned in chapter 1.

Yolande d'Aragon, René's mother also held court there till she died in 1442.

In the 16th century **Saumur** was a predominantly protestant city. Some years after the St. Bartholomew's massacre in 1576, Henri, the King of Navarre, who had just escaped from Paris, found sanctuary there and hastened to renounce the Catholicism that he had converted to under pressure from King Charles IX (he had been told to choose between "the Mass and Death").

In 1589 he signed a Treaty with King Henri III, who gave him **Saumur** as a secure place, offering a crossing over the Loire.

Loches: Perched on a rocky spur, situated in the confines of Poitou, Touraine and Berry, these natural attributes gave **Loches** a great strategic importance in the Middle Ages. The great square keep was built by the Counts of Anjou in the 11th century on even earlier foundations. After the death of Henry II Plantagenet, while Richard Lionheart was in captivity on his return from the Third Crusade, King Philippe-Auguste of France conspired with John Lackland, Richard's notorious brother and took **Loches**.

After his liberation Richard, seriously annoyed, rushed there and recaptured the castle in 3 hours with a surprise attack. Ten years later Philippe-Auguste took it back in not so spectacular fashion – his siege lasted a whole year! Since then the fortress has been a Royal stronghold and a secure French State Prison.

The Royal residence was built later, the works started at the end of the 14th century as an extension of a watch tower which is known today as the Agnes Sorel tower. Part of the building dates from the medieval period, another part from the Renaissance.

A diminutive oratory, in the so called Flamboyant style, was built for Anne of Brittany and decorated with her symbols – the ermine of Brittany and the girdle of St. Francis.

Chambord: The Counts of Blois, great hunters, built a fortress in this game filled forest. It was demolished by François I in 1519 and he then proceeded to build in its place a masterpiece, which would become the hallmark of his reign, and the scale of which, would overshadow even Versailles. With its 440 rooms it is the biggest of the Loire châteaux.

At a time when the Treasury was empty and the King didn't even have the funds to pay the ransoms for his sons, held as hostages by the Spanish, a time when he had to resort to desperate measures, to melt his subjects' silver and to help himself to church assets, François stubbornly pursued the work on his château.

The result is dazzling: this white edifice, consisting of numerous stylish tours, turrets and chimneys takes your breath away, when it suddenly appears at the end of a wooded avenue in all its glory. The effect is particularly striking at sunset.

Chambord truly represents the humanist dream come true of the radiant city, exquisite in each and every detail on the exterior (an impressive group of some 800 capitals, 365 chimneys, spires and bell turrets), as well as in the interior where we can marvel at the numerous staircases (14 great staircases and about 70 minor ones), of which the most wonderful is the double helix staircase at the heart of the edifice. There are beautifully decorated ceilings, elaborate fireplaces, the work of great craftsmen to marvel at and then all those numerous nooks and crannies to explore.

Another outstanding feature is the Italian inspired roof terrace, where the court spent most of its time, watching the beginning and the end of the hunts, various tournaments and festivities.

Chambord today belongs to the State and is included in the list of UNESCO.

Chenonceau, one of the loveliest of the châteaux, is situated on the river Cher, a tributary of the Loire. The present château was built 1513 – 1521 by Thomas Bohier, collector of taxes for Charles VIII, Louis XII and François I. It passed to the King – Bohier's son had to give it up to cover the debts of his father who had embezzled funds from the Royal Treasury. Nowadays **Chenonceau** has become known as the château of 6 women and one can clearly feel the feminine touch. Who were these women?

The wife of Thomas Bohier, Katherine (remembered as the Builder) oversaw the works while her husband was fighting wars in Italy with the king's army. To her we owe the concept of the château and its style.

Diane de Poitiers (the Ever-Beautiful) received it as a gift from her Royal lover, Henri II; she had a splendid garden laid out and a bridge thrown over the Cher to connect the château with the far bank of the river. She drew plenty of funds from the tax of 20 *livres* on every church bell, levied by Henri, so she was not short of cash and could follow every whim she had.

Catherine de Medici (the Magnificent), the wife of Henri II settled scores with Diane after his untimely death at a tournament. She made the Royal mistress give up **Chenonceau** in exchange for **Chaumont,** a masterstroke to humiliate her rival without appearing bitter. Catherine de Medici with her love for splendour, pursued improving the place on a grand scale – a park was laid out, a two storey gallery was mounted on the bridge, extensive outbuildings were erected.

Louise de Lorraine (the Inconsolable), the wife of Henri III, inherited **Chenonceau** from her mother-in-law Catherine de Medici. After the assassination of her husband, devastated, the poor woman retired to the château. She had her furniture covered in black damask, her ceilings painted in black with white crowns of thorns and Franciscan girdles as the only decoration. In such morbid surroundings she spent the remaining years of her life.

After her death the château was neglected and gradually fell into disrepair – beloved by the Valois, it was not valued by the Bourbons. The last King who stayed there was Louis XIV (the Sun- King) in 1650 (interestingly on 14th July).

Chenonceau remained in slumber until 1733 when General Dupin acquired it. Then Madame Dupin (Lover of Letters) took charge of it. There she entertained, amongst others: Voltaire, Marivaux, Montesquieu. Jean-Jacques Rousseau was the tutor of her son and wrote "Emile" for his benefit. Madame Dupin was a favourite with the local peasants, so the château survived the revolution.

Madame de Pelouze (Lover of Antiquity) acquired it in the 19th century and entirely restored it.

The château is now owned by the Menier family who had to restore it again after two world wars worth of damage, but it has now regained its former glory and is open to the public.

Chaumont was built in the 10th century by the Counts of Blois to protect the town against the Counts of Anjou; it later passed into the hands of the Amboise family by marriage. Burnt down in 1455 by Louis XI to punish Pierre d'Amboise, it was rebuilt between 1465 and 1510 by the latter, his eldest son and his grandson.

The castle was later acquired by Catherine de Medici and exchanged for Diane de Poitiers' **Chenonceau**, though it's doubtful that she obtained it with that purpose in mind, as is now claimed. It is important to note, having in mind its position, the domain had substantial revenue to recommend it to a potential buyer.

The name **Chaumont** comes from a volcano (*Chaud Mont*) thus the emblem that can be seen on the façade, along with others – like the initials of the Amboises – interlaced "C"s for Charles and Catherine, the intertwined "D"s for Diane de Poitiers or the hunting horn, bow and quiver, symbolising Diane, the Huntress.

In fact Diane de Poitiers didn't stay there long (she preferred to retire to her château at Anet) and it's ironic that neither of the two women found it to their taste.

The château looks like a real fortress, perched high up, commanding the Loire. There are superb views of the valley to be had from the terrace. We can enjoy this panorama today because the northern wing that used to be there was demolished in the 18th century when the château lost something of its military allure, but gained as a residence of ease and comfort.

Nantes The château was rebuilt and strengthened from 1466 onwards by François II, Duke of Brittany and his daughter Anne. It was a citadel of ducal power, conceived as a stronghold to ensure the independence of Brittany during the time of Louis XI and his successors. Anne of Brittany continued her father's work.

The defensive system of the fortress consists of seven towers with the typical Breton pyramidal shaped machicolations, connected by a curtain wall and deep wide ditches which could be flooded if the need arose.

Once in the interior courtyard the contrast between the fortified exterior walls and the elegant residential part, built of white lime stone and lavishly decorated, becomes apparent.

Le Grand Logis was realised by Duke François II and served as a residence for him and for his court. *La Tour de la courronne d'Or* (the Golden Crown Tower) next to it was also built by him and finished by his daughter Anne; it owes its name to the nearby well that has a wrought iron wellhead in the shape of a ducal crown. The *Palais Ducal* and other parts were reconstructed later, while the oldest remaining part called *Le Vieux Donjon* (The Ancient Keep), built by Jean IV Duke of Brittany, dates from the 14th century.

Plessis-lès-Tours (La Riche, Tours), a Royal abode during the time of Louis XI – the château was built for him when he based himself in Touraine, while his wife, Queen Charlotte, lived in Amboise. The château, which couldn't compete with its more eye-catching neighbours, is now almost forgotten as is its most illustrious occupant. Today only one wing remains of it and even that was entirely modified at the end of the 19th century; only the cylindrical stairwell was preserved in its original state. Miser as he was, Louis XI didn't splash out the way his predecessors or successors did, but still he had there a well appointed Renaissance style residence built around a central courtyard, as we can see from an old engraving. In its hey-day the château had a large contingent of visitors and had seen many an important guest; not least because of Tours being the venue for the States General in 1468, 1484, 1506. In 1589 it witnessed the fateful meeting between Henri III and Henri of Navarre when they decided to unite forces against the Catholic League. It's a pity that a historical building like this should be so neglected. It's not open to the public anymore. It's not well signposted either, presumably to discourage curious tourists. From all appearances it seems that the building is now used as a rehearsal studio for a theatre company.

Langeais. A fortress was originally raised there by that tireless builder Foulque Nerra, the Count of Anjou (the ruins of the ancient keep are still preserved) and extended by Richard Lionheart. But his rival King Phillipe Auguste of France obtained it, amongst others, from John Lackland.

During the 100 Years War it was taken by the English who kept it until 1428 and then agreed to leave it for a handsome ransom of 2000 *ecus* and on the condition that the *"castel soit rasé et abbatu à l'exception de la grosse tour"*. Accordingly it was demolished with only the big tower left standing. Louis XI who realised its strategic potential, had the château rebuilt (1465), under the direction of Jean Bourré (the Treasurer of the King) and the aspect of this edifice, a perfect example of a medieval castle with high walls, round towers, machicolations, a moat and a drawbridge, has remained unaltered ever since.

However viewed from the interior courtyard it looks less severe, opened to the gardens, in what is known as pure gothic - flamboyant style, featuring mullioned dormer windows, aimed at comfort, not defence; to provide a pleasant sojourn as the residence of a great 15th century lord should be.

Inside it has also been beautifully furnished in the 15th century style thanks to the efforts of the last owner, who bequeathed it to the Institute of France in 1904.

The marriage of Anne and Charles VIII, which took place here in 1491, is brought back to life with an impressive recreation using wax figures of the participants in the ceremony.

Châteaudun. Initially built by the Counts of Blois, sold later to Louis, the Duke of Orleans, it was later given to his bastard son Jean, Count of Dunois (in 1439) by his half brother, Charles of Orleans. Dunois did more work on it, which was pursued by his successors, as it was the seat of the Counts of Dunois. Châteaudun is situated above the meandering Loir, a tributary of the Loire. From the outside it has the appearance of a fortress, which it undoubtedly was during the medieval period. The impressive 12th century keep is 31m high (102ft) it was one of the first round keeps and is well preserved.

Standing in the main courtyard, we face a stately manor. Dunois built the Gothic wing which is now named after him, and a chapel, *Saint Chapelle* and his successors built the so called Longueville wing.

Beaugency. A fortified town since medieval times. The 11th century rectangular keep is still standing; the fortified mansion, today known as château Dunois was built as his main residence by the Bastard of Orleans; he received the lordship of **Beaugency**, marrying Marie de Harcourt the year he became the Count of Dunois and then started the reconstruction works.

In those times **Beaugency** was of far greater importance, commanding the only bridge on the Loire between Blois and Orleans (there were 7 bridges in total between Gien and Angers). That's why during the 100 Years War the English attacked the town and held it 4 times (in 1356, 1412, 1421, 1428). It was Joan of Arc who delivered it in 1429 after her victory at Orleans (to get to Orleans, she had to cross the Loire in a boat at Chécy).

There is an interesting legend about the **Beaugency** Bridge that has inspired James Joyce for the story "The Cat and the Devil" (written initially for his grandson). It's believed to have been built in one night only by the Devil himself, who knew that the local people badly needed it but did not have the means to pay for it. He offered it to them for free, on the condition that the first one who ventured across the bridge would be his. The Abbot (or according to some versions the Mayor) got a cat and setting it at the head of the bridge, splashed a bucket full of cold water over it. The cat dashed across the bridge straight into the arms of the Devil, who was not at all impressed. "You are not very nice people," he said to the crowd that was gathered around, "you are nothing but cats." That's why to this day they refer to the people of **Beaugency** as the cats from **Beaugency**.

The Devils Tower, dating from the 11th -12th centuries, protecting the head of the legendary bridge over the Loire, was restored in 1460 at the bidding of the Count of Dunois. He lived there for 17 years. Louis XI visited Dunois at **Beaugency** on 4/10/1461 on his way back from his coronation in Reims and his stay in Paris.

Azay-le-Brulé/Azay-le-Rideau A fortress was built there in 1119 by Ridel d'Azay. Burnt by the future Charles VII in 1418, the lordship of Azay was later acquired by Gilles Berthelot (in 1510), a General Tax Collector and, afterwards, Treasurer of France during the time of François I. Obviously he wasn't short of funds as he started a major reconstruction of the château in the contemporary Italian style. The result is this architectural masterpiece, floating in the waters of the river Indre, a lovely melange of French traditions and innovative details imported from Italy.

Berthelot didn't have much time to enjoy it. He was a protégé of Semblançay, the Financial Secretary of the Kingdom, who was accused of corruption and executed in 1527. Frightened that he might be implicated too, Berthelot fled, leaving his wife behind. François I then gave the château to one of his comrades in arms from his Italian campaigns. During the French Revolution it was acquired by the Biencourt family who gradually restored the château to its former glory.

The State bought it from the last Marquis at the beginning of the 20th century.

Montsoreau. Built in the 15th century by Jean de Chambes, counsellor of Charles VII, it is connected with the mistress of the Duke de Berry, the League of Public Weal and Louis XI, who allegedly disposed of them both. There is confusion as to who the husband of this notorious lady was. She was supposed to be the widow of Pierre d'Amboise (house of Amboise-Chaumont), who was punished for his participation in the league, his château de Chaumont was demolished; although reconstructed later by his successors.

In fact she was the second wife of his cousin Louis, who was involved in the 100 Years War, fighting alongside Joan of Arc, but was imprisoned for his involvement in a plot against La Trémoille, a Chamberlain and a favourite of Charles VII.

Hundred years later another melodrama took place in the chateau. This time it involved the wife of the Lord of Montsoreau. Her lover, Bussy, was murdered by the deceived husband.

Montrichard was built, true to form by Foulque Nerra, the Count of Anjou as one of many strongholds (he left behind about hundred castles, dungeons and fortified abbeys) in his fight with the Count of Blois. Hugues d'Amboise seized it in 1109 and so during the Middle Ages it belonged to the Counts of Amboise, together with **Amboise** itself. Louis d'Amboise lost it (see château **Montsoreau**). It was confiscated, together with the château **Amboise** (and the title of Amboise) as a result of Louis d'Amboise's unfortunate attempt to kidnap La Tremoille; since when it became Crown property. The marriage of the future Louis XII with Jeanne de Valois, the daughter of Louis XI, was celebrated there, in Ste Croix chapel.

Brissac. Originally a fortress was built here, by, who else, but the formidable Foulque Nerra. Then in the 15th century Pierre de Brezé, minister under both Charles VII and Louis XI, acquired it and undertook a major reconstruction. During the reign of François I it changed hands again and became the property of René de Cossé who acquired also the title Count of Brissac. During the Wars of Religion, his grandson Charles, a governor of Paris, opened the city gates to King Henri IV in 1594, which earned him the rank of a Marshal and later a ducal crown. The Duke of Brissac started to build a grand new chateau on top of the ruins of the old one (which was badly damaged during the Wars of Religion). The enormous expense all but ruined him and, with the works put on hold by his death and never resumed, the château was left unfinished with two of the old towers which were due to be demolished, still standing. This is how we find it today: an impressive edifice which, with its seven storeys, is considered to be the tallest in the Loire valley if not in the whole of France. It displays a façade partly medieval and partly Renaissance; two massive, fortified towers clasping between them a Renaissance style residence.

Also of note:
Villandry was built by Jean de Breton, Secretary of state to François I; of that original chateau only the keep remains. Today known for its Renaissance gardens, redone the way they would have been in the 16th century.
Plessis-Macé is an old fortress, started in the 11th century by a certain Macé; it became the property of Louis de Beaumont, a Chamberlain to Louis XI in the middle of the 15th century; the interior courtyard was much embellished and improved in the 15th century to become a fortified manor house.
Plessis-Bourré was built at the end of the 15th century by Jean Bourré (the Treasurer of King Louis XI), who oversaw the works at château **Langeais** and decided to build one for himself too. On the outside it looks like a real fortress with its big towers, wide moats and a drawbridge, but the interior is of a rich manor house.
Ussé is an ancient fortress, which was acquired by a Touraine family, the Bueils, who distinguished themselves during the 100 Years War and wanted to have a residence to match their status. One of them, who married a daughter of Charles VII and Agnes Sorel, sold the château to the Espinays, a Breton family who supplied chamberlains and cup bearers to the duke of Brittany, Louis XI and Charles VIII. The château often changed hands during the centuries.

Overlooking the Indre River with high cliffs in the background, château Ussé is the ultimate fairy tale castle. No surprise that Charles Perrault, the 17th century writer, was so taken by it when he stayed there, that he was inspired (or so they say) for the setting of his Sleeping Beauty, one of the tales he included in his Histories or Tales of Long Ago with Morals: Tales of Mother Goose, that he is best remembered for.

Vendôme – now only the ruins of the ancient château remind us of its former magnitude.

Royal Genealogy

The House of Valois is founded by Philippe, Count of Valois; his father was Charles of Valois, the brother of King Philippe IV the Fair (*Philippe IV le Bel*)

The Royal House of Valois (direct Valois)

Philippe VI the Fortunate (*le Fortuné*), nephew of King Philippe, the Fair (1328-1350)

Jean II the Good (*Jean II le Bon*), (1350-1364), his son

Charles V the Wise (*le Sage*), (1364-1380), the eldest son of Jean II

Charles VI the Beloved/the Mad (*le Bien Aimé/ le Fou*), (1380-1422), son of Charles V

Charles VII the Victorious/the Well Served (le *Victorieux/ le Bien Servi*), (1422-1461), the son of Charles VI

Louis XI the Prudent/ the Universal Spider (*le Prudent/ l'Universelle Aragne*), (1461-1483), son of Charles VII

Charles VIII the Affable (*l'Affable*), (1483-1498), son of Louis XI, the 7th and last King of this branch.

The Valois/Orléans Branch

Louis I, Duke of Orléans and Count of Valois, (1372-1407), son of King Charles V of France

Charles I, Duke of Orleans (1407-1465, count of Valois and Blois), son of Louis.

Louis XII, King of France (1498-1515), The Father of the People (*le Père du Peuple*), son of Charles, Duke of Orleans

Valois-Orleans-Angoulême Branch

Jean of Orleans, Count of Angoulême, son of Louis I, Duke of Orleans

Charles of Orleans, Count of Angoulême

François I, King of France (1515-1547), the Chivalrous king/Prince of Renaissance, son of Charles, Count of Angoulême

Henri II (1547-1559), King of France, son of King François I

François II (1559-1560), King of France, the eldest son of Henri II

Charles IX (1560-1574), King of France, son of Henri II

Henri III (1574-1589), King of France, son of Henri II, the last King of the Valois Dynasty

The Royal House of Lancaster, England

The Royal House of Lancaster stems from the 3rd son of King Edward III of England, John of Gaunt. This Prince married a rich heiress, Blanche of Lancaster, who made him one of the wealthiest landowners of England. His son Henry of Bolingbroke deposed his cousin King Richard II (and very likely had him murdered), and reigned England under the name of Henry IV.

Henry IV (1399-1413) had earlier married Mary de Bohun who gave him six children but did not live to become a Queen, dying in childbirth 5 years prior to her husband's ascent to the throne. Their eldest son succeeded him to the throne.

Henry V (1413-1422); resumed the 100 Years War and had certain success, winning several battles and notably the Battle of Agincourt; allied himself with the House of Burgundy, a cadet line of the Royal House of Valois. He married Catherine Valois of France, the daughter of the French King Charles VI the Mad and was recognised as his heir thus ousting the Dauphin Charles. However Henry V died before his father-in-law. His infant son Henry succeeded him on the English throne as Henry VI. Later on Henry's widow, Catherine got involved with and, possibly, secretly married, Owen Tudor of Wales thus becoming the grandmother of Henry VII of England who founded the Tudor Dynasty. Other descendants of theirs include King Charles I of England and his opponent Oliver Cromwell, King Juan Carlos of Spain as well as Queen Elizabeth II, the current reigning monarch of the UK and the rest of the Commonwealth.

Henry VI (1422-1461; 1470-1471), son of Henry V, suffered from bouts of insanity, not unlike his maternal grandfather Charles VI the Mad; Henry VI married Marguerite of Anjou, the daughter of Good King René and niece of his rival King Charles VII of France. Charles VII agreed to this marriage on the condition that he was not to pay the customary dowry, but was to receive Anjou and Maine instead, a move not very popular in England when it became public knowledge. Gradually Henry (and Marguerite who influenced him) lost all of their French possessions (apart from Calais) and got involved in the War of the Roses. Finally Henry was deposed by the York supporters and as his son did not outlive him, his rival, Edward of York became a King under the name of Edward IV of England.

Valois-Burgundian Branch – Dukes of Burgundy

Philippe the Bold (le Hardi) (1364-1404), brother of King Charles V of France

John the Fearless (1404-1419); murdered his cousin Louis, Duke of Orleans; murdered in turn by the Armagnac clan on the Dauphin's (the future Charles VII) orders.

Philippe the Good (1419-1467), son of John the Fearless; allied himself with Henry V of England under the Treaty of Troyes. In 1430 his troops captured Joan of Arc and later handed her over to the English. In 1435 his alliance with the English was broken as he recognised Charles VII as King of France. His peace with Charles VII was however broken again in 1439 when he joined the *Praguerie*, aligning himself on the side of the Dauphin Louis (future Louis XI).

Charles the Reckless (1467-1477), son of Philippe the Good; was on friendly terms with the Dauphin Louis, but later on he sided with the League of Public Weal; his third wife was Margaret of York, a distant cousin of his, for they were both descendants of John of Gaunt of England, thus enforcing his renewed alliance with the English. Louis XI of France did everything to prevent this marriage but in vain. Margaret didn't give any children to her husband but took care of his daughter Mary from his second wife Isabel of Bourbon and later, when Mary died – of her children. The Duke died at the siege of Nancy.

Mary of Burgundy (the Rich) (1457-1482), the only child of Charles the Reckless; her godfather was the Dauphin in exile at the time, the future King Louis XI of France, who after the death of her father sought her hand for his son Charles, 13 years her junior, so he could lay his hands on the Low Countries; advised by her stepmother Margaret of York, Mary declined the French alliance; married instead Maximilian I, the Holy Roman Emperor of the House of Habsburg. She died at the age of 25 after a fall from her horse while hunting with falcons, accompanied by her husband. Later Maximilian married by proxy the Duchess Anne of Brittany but before he managed to meet his young wife, was ousted by King Charles VIII of France, (the son of Louis XI), who married her instead. As a result the Emperor lost Brittany, but recovered the lands that were given as a dowry for his daughter Margaret, who had been betrothed to the French King when she was 3 years old and had remained at the French court ever since, but sent away later on after he married Anne.

www.ingramcontent.com/pod-product-compliance
Ingram Content Group UK Ltd.
Pitfield, Milton Keynes, MK11 3LW, UK
UKHW041436180426
11947UKWH00007B/476